THE MERSEYSIDE SCOTS

A Study of an Expatriate Community

by

Alasdair Munro and Duncan Sim

The History and Society of Merseyside Series is a joint venture between the School of Social Science, Liverpool John Moores University, the School of History, University of Liverpool and Countyvise Limited, publishers of studies in local history.

The aim of the venture is to publish research material which will be of interest to a wide spectrum of readers on Merseyside and elsewhere so developing greater links between two of the higher institutions of the city, with the community of the region. The series provides a publishing outlet for outstanding dissertations or projects by final year and MA students and for appropriate material from other sources.

First published 2001 by Liver Press,
14 Appin Road, Birkenhead, Merseyside, CH41 9HH

Copyright © 2001 Alasdair Munro and Duncan Sim

The right of Alasdair Munro and Duncan Sim to be identified as the authors of this work have been asserted by them in accordance with the Copyright, Design and Patents Act 1988.

British Library Cataloguing in Publication Data.
A Catalogue record for this book is available from the British Library.

ISBN 1 871201 10 1

Printed and Typeset by Birkenhead Press Limited,
14 Appin Road, Birkenhead, Merseyside, CH41 9HH

DEDICATION

To our Families

Also published by Liver Press:

Pat Ayers · *Liverpool Women at War 1939-45.*

Anthony Miller · *Poverty Deserved?*
Relieving the Poor in Victorian Liverpool

Joan Boyce · *Pillowslips and Gasmasks.*
Liverpool's Wartime Evacuation

Maria Lin Wong · *Chinese Liverpudlians.*
A History of the Chinese Community in Liverpool

Sam Davies · *Genuinely Seeking Work.*
Pete Gill · *Mass unemployment on Merseyside in the 1930s*
Linda Grant
Martyn Nightingale
Ron Noon
Andy Shallice

Andrea Murphy · *From the Empire to the Rialto.*
Rascism and Reaction in Liverpool 1918-1948

Michael Lavalette · *Solidarity on the Waterfront.*
Jane Kennedy · *The Liverpool Lockout 1995-96*

Pat Ayers · *The Liverpool Docklands.*
Life and Work in Athol Street.

Cpl. George Carruthers, Liverpool Scottish
Grandfather of the authors

CONTENTS

Foreword and Acknowledgements

FOREWORD AND ACKNOWLEDGEMENTS

This short book has no pretensions to be a full history of Scots on Merseyside, so much as an attempt to show that the area owes a great deal to a national group who have not been as readily identifiable as others. The Irish were predominantly Roman Catholic and, in the nineteenth century, were concentrated in one particular area of Liverpool. The Welsh tended to attend Welsh language churches and to be concentrated in certain professions such as teaching, building and retailing. Scots, on the other hand, lived throughout the city and were found in most trades and professions. Even in Scotland itself, church history is a series of secessions and schisms, so that Scots did not identify with particular churches, as other national groups did.

The authors' awareness of the Scottish community on Merseyside comes largely from their related families and it is probably appropriate to indicate their relationship to certain people referred to in the text:

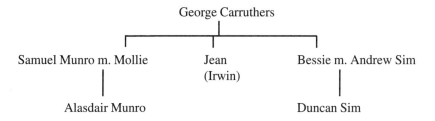

We have received a lot of help from various individuals in the preparation of this book, including Mrs. Hazel Bishop, Mr. George Penman, Mr. Tom Graham, Mr. Eddie Roose, Miss Nancy Wright, Mr. Rob Blackmore, Mr. William McKay, Mrs. E. Adam, Mr. N. Mason, Lt. Col. Graeme Davidson, and especially Mrs. Jean Kewley J.P., and Mr. Dennis Reeves. We are also grateful to library staff in Liverpool, Birkenhead, Glasgow and Edinburgh for assistance and advice.

January 1998.

CHAPTER ONE

Introduction

Introduction

Scotland, like Ireland, has long been a country of emigration and indeed, both countries have large expatriate societies scattered across the globe. People of Scots origin may therefore be found in all continents and particularly in countries that were once part of the British Empire. The Scottish presence is revealed in various ways - in local surnames, in place names, perhaps in the existence of a Caledonian Society - while particular concentrations of expatriates may be indicated in more significant ways. The large Scottish settlement in eastern Canada has resulted in the province itself being known as "Nova Scotia".

Much has been written about expatriate Scottish societies overseas and there are various organisations and publications designed to maintain these overseas links. There appear, however, to be few studies of expatriate Scottish societies within the United Kingdom itself, although a number of English cities have had a significant Scottish presence. This particular volume focuses on such a society - the expatriate Scots of Merseyside.

The Causes of Migration

Studies of Scottish emigration reveal something of a paradox. During the nineteenth century, emigration from Scotland was part of a broader movement of people out of Europe - frequently in the direction of the Americas. Outward movement from Scotland was consistently high throughout this period and, of sixteen western and central European countries studied by Baines [1], three - Ireland, Scotland and Norway - dominated the 'league table'. Perhaps not unexpectedly, Ireland was usually the country with the greatest number of emigrants, although in 1913, Scotland had a higher rate of emigration than any other European country. It should also be noted that this study specifically excluded Scottish emigration to England.

The paradox of Scottish emigration lay in the nature of the exporting country. Almost all major groups of emigrants originated in agrarian economies which, in addition to Ireland and Norway, included Italy, Spain and Portugal.

> Yet the economic circumstances were entirely different in Scotland. Emigration.......expanded rapidly just as indigenous employment opportunities became more available and standards of living rose moderately in the later nineteenth century. The transformation of the

economy enabled additional numbers to be fed, clothed and employed. Scottish population as a result rose from 1,265,380 in 1755 to 4,472,103 in 1901. But it was precisely in this period that more and more decided to leave. Between 1825 and 1938, 2,332,608 people departed Scotland for overseas destinations. No other industrial society in Europe experienced such a haemorrhage [2].

That is not to say that, within Scotland, there was no agrarian emigration; on the contrary, large numbers of people moved out from the Highlands, particularly in the eighteenth and early nineteenth centuries. Population growth within the area led to demands on local agriculture which could not be met, the situation worsening after failures of the potato crop in the 1840s. Bluntly, the area could not support the numbers of people living there and, as a result, various Government reports began to refer to the Highlands as 'the congested districts'. Many households were forced to move southwards, to the industrial Lowlands, to England or overseas. The situation might have been different had industrial development occurred in the Highlands but the area possessed neither coal nor iron ore, the ingredients which might have made such industrialisation possible.

The relatively poor crop yields led many landowners to look for alternative uses for the land and the early nineteenth century saw the introduction of extensive sheep farming. Crofters in many parts of Scotland were cleared to make way for the sheep, some being relocated in planned settlements on the coast, where fishing industries expanded; others simply emigrated. Some estates were turned over to deer farming with the same results.

Generally speaking, however, Central Scotland expanded considerably in this period and industries such as mining, steelmaking, shipbuilding and engineering offered great opportunities for employment. A further paradox of Scottish emigration therefore is the fact that, while many Scots were leaving the country, migration into Scotland was actually on the increase. Some of this migration was from Ireland and the number of Irish born in Scotland reached 7.2 per cent of the population in 1851. Some migrants came from England because, as Cage [3] has pointed out, the development of Central Scotland was an integral part of the Industrial Revolution. Industrial areas throughout the UK were interdependent, relying on each other for labour, raw materials, finance and markets.

Some Scottish industries, however, did decline. One of the best examples is handloom weaving, which moved towards extinction in the mid-nineteenth century. Thus, while new arrivals from the Highlands - or indeed Ireland - were moving into some industries, Scottish weavers moved out, often to go overseas [4]. Thus the migration which affected all parts of Scotland was an extremely complex process.

As well as circumstances which 'pushed' people towards emigration, there were of course 'pull' factors which encouraged households to move to particular areas. Probably the most significant of these was the existence of job opportunities in expanding manufacturing industry and many areas throughout England, but particularly in the north, would have been attractive in this respect. The expansion of Tyneside, for example, provided opportunities for employment for migrants from the Scottish Borders [5]. A study by Brock [6] of migration from the Scottish counties shows that all the counties from which more than 10 per cent of the population had moved to England and Wales were in the Borders region. Although the Borders had relatively high agricultural wages, they were still lower than North East England where wages were amongst the highest in Britain.

Although Merseyside is clearly much further from Scotland than Tyneside, Dennis suggests [7] that it would have attracted Scots (and Cumbrian) migrants because of the absence of any major opportunities in the intervening area. In contrast, migrants from the south of England tended to move indirectly, sometimes gaining employment en route. Motives for migration were clearly variable. Economic motives may be inferred for many of the migrants although, as Pooley and Doherty have shown in relation to Welsh migrants to England [8], economic advancement did not immediately follow. Perhaps the main economic benefits were experienced by those entering the labour market for the first time but, in the longer term, the larger labour markets in England could have offered a better range of employment prospects. Many migrants certainly advanced in employment terms, although Jackson suggests that the popular image of the Irish as labourers who stayed as such had some truth in it [9].

In the case of the Scots, part of the influx of migrants to Merseyside would have been by entrepreneurs seeking to invest in English business, as well as by Scottish workers. A city like Liverpool, with its developing commercial and shipping interests would have been quite a magnet for Scots businessmen and it is unsurprising that so many chose to take advantage of the opportunities available. The role of Scots in the port and commercial life of Merseyside is discussed in more detail in Chapter Five.

There were, too, opportunities in the professions, because the Scots education system in the nineteenth century was undoubtedly superior to that of England. The Scottish universities in particular were strong, with a curriculum based especially on science and medicine. Thus many Scots in England had moved south to become lawyers, officers, politicians and, especially doctors [10]. Scots played an enormously significant role in medicine on Merseyside and this is discussed further in Chapter Four.

Many Scots, simply, liked to be mobile. Even before 1750, there was a tradition of movement by Scots into the colonies and cultural factors, notably their religious and educational background, may have led Scots to seek self advancement more readily than others. This may have led to a greater propensity to emigrate, in search of appropriate opportunities [11]. Some Scots opted for mobile forms of employment, such as hawking or peddling; 'in Manchester at the beginning of this century, "Scotsman" could still mean a hawker peddling wares from door to door' [12].

Despite the paradoxes and complexities involved in Scottish emigration, it is clear that movement out of Scotland in the nineteenth century took place at a time when, in the industrial areas at least, the economy was expanding. The situation, however, changed after the First World War. Firstly, the fishing industry, expanded after the Highland Clearances, began itself to decline and the herring industry in particular all but collapsed. There was therefore renewed emigration, this time from the west and east coast fishing ports. Secondly, the Depression of the 1930s and the closure or stagnation of some industries such as Clyde shipbuilding, similarly led many Scots families to look elsewhere for work. Once again, many went overseas, although some moved south to England.

Some Scots, in their quest for work, accepted a role as strike breakers, a role also sometimes played by the Irish [13]. Cage, for example, refers to a strike at Bridgewater Foundry in 1836, which was broken by importing sixty-four men from Scotland. Relatives followed them so that the majority of workers at the Foundry became Scottish [14].

A good Merseyside example is provided by the influx of Scots into the local police force. At one time, the Liverpool City Police had a deliberate policy of recruiting from outside the city, advertising particularly in Welsh and Scots newspapers. Pay was relatively poor - in 1919, a constable's wage was £2. 13s, compared with a dock gateman's £3 8s - but many Scots miners and men from rural areas felt that it still represented a betterment of their working conditions. Some rural Scots found difficulty in making themselves understood; on one occasion when an Orcadian policeman was giving evidence, the magistrate asked for an interpreter [15]. There was a particular influx of Scots into the police force, after the dismissal of those who had joined the 1919 Liverpool Police Strike; a number of vacancies were created and wages improved [16].

Finally, in more recent years, a number of Scots have moved to Merseyside as football players or managers, not because of a lack of opportunities in Scotland perhaps, but because of greater financial rewards with big clubs like Liverpool or Everton. Since the 1950s, migration to Merseyside by Scots seems to be of much less significance than previously, as shown in Chapter Two. The influx of Scottish footballers to the area may therefore have been important in preserving a Scottish profile on Merseyside. Appendix One lists the various Scottish internationalists who have played for Merseyside clubs and the list is quite a long one.

The Scots on Merseyside

Although migration to the cities was a significant feature of Victorian urbanisation, at a local level the process has been only partially documented. According to Holmes [17],

> Liverpool, for example, has accommodated Africans, Chinese and Jews as well as a traditionally large Irish element, but a general history of immigrants in Liverpool concentrating on numbers, social structure, varieties of cultural life, and their complex range of relationships with the receiving society has never been attempted.

Early studies of migration to Merseyside tended to focus on Census data, using birthplace tables to identify the extent of immigration to the area. The work of Lawton [18] and Pickett [19] showed how the conurbation's growth was heavily dependent on the inward movement of people, particularly from Ireland. Indeed, perhaps because of the scale of Irish migration, it has commanded the most attention. Later work has focused on specific communities within Merseyside - and particularly within Liverpool. Some writers, such as Dennis [20] and Pooley [21], have explored levels of segregation within migrant communities and the existence of areas of the city, dominated by one particular migrant group.

There have now been a number of studies of the Irish in Britain, for example by Jackson [22], O'Connor [23], and Buckland and Belchem [24], all of which deal in varying degrees of detail with the Merseyside perspective. There have also been studies of the sectarianism which has subsequently arisen, as a result of the Irish presence in Liverpool, by Bohstedt [25] and Waller [26]. The Welsh have also been studied, for example in Pooley and Doherty's [27] detailed work on the movement of Welsh families to English towns, using Census enumerators' books, as well as in Roberts's [28] work on Welsh influences in Liverpool industry.

Most recently, there has been considerable research on the black and minority ethnic communities on Merseyside. Some of this has taken a historical approach, tracing the history of black communities in Liverpool, linked in to its mercantile past, for example the work of Murphy [29] and Law and Henfey [30]. There have also been studies of individual communities such as the black Afro-Caribbeans, by Frost [31] and Christian [32], and of the Chinese by Wong [33] and Lynn [34]. Some of this work has explored social and political perspectives of ethnicity, as well as purely historical ones. One of the most significant pieces of research in this regard is by Ben-Tovim et al [35], examining the role of racial and ethnic politics in the political life of the city; Liverpool was one of their case studies. Finally, the Commission for Racial Equality has added to the material available on minority communities through its studies and investigations of discrimination and disadvantage [36].

Although there are studies of Scottish migration overseas and of Scottish expatriate communities, there appears to be very little work on Scottish communities in England, despite their being regarded as culturally distinctive. As Lawton and Pooley point out [37]:

> Among the many migrants into Victorian cities, some were set apart by easily identifiable social and cultural characteristics. Most obvious were the Irish but European migrants, especially Jews, also formed cohesive and distinctive communities in many towns, whilst Welsh and Scottish migrants were sometimes perceived as distinctive cultural groups in England and vice-versa.

Census figures furnish us with the overall statistics, from 1851 onwards, and give some indication of where, within towns and cities, the migrant groups were located. Chapter Two shows that, within Liverpool, Scots migrants did not cluster into particular parts of the city and there was no 'Scottish Quarter' - in contrast to the Irish and Welsh. This may account for the fact that the Scots' contribution to Merseyside life has been relatively poorly documented, although it is also suggested that the Scots would be less likely to appear in official records from the period:

> The main reason why so little is known about the Scots migrants is, perhaps, that they less frequently required poor relief than the Irish. This was noticed both at Manchester and at Liverpool, though in each town there was a considerable Scots colony [38].

Indeed, in the nineteenth century, commentators drew attention to the difference between the Irish and other migrants. The Irish tended to be labourers and were not particularly upwardly mobile. In 1834, there were 3,500 Irish labourers working in the docks in Liverpool and by 1851, probably one half to three quarters of all dock labour was Irish. The women tended to find employment in domestic service. In 1851, 12 per cent of those employed in the merchants' houses of Liverpool's Abercromby Square area were Irish [39].

Unlike many of the Irish and Welsh, the Scots were not distinguished from their English hosts by religion and language. Some researchers have focused on the Irish precisely because they could often be so distinguished:

> The Irish were set apart from the population at large by religion (usually), language (often) and way of life, and their perceived willingness to accept low wages and undercut English labour was especially divisive [40].

The separate religion of most Irish families - Roman Catholicism - led to antagonism within Merseyside and, during the Irish Troubles of the 1920s, there was a considerable development of associations affiliated to the Orange Order within the area [41]. Roman Catholic children had their own schools, emphasising the differences from the 'host' population. It should of course be stressed, however, that many Irish migrants - particularly from Ulster - were not Catholic and indeed, as Presbyterians, had many links with Scotland. Some of these families became active within the Orange Order on Merseyside.

Many Welsh were also distinguished by their separate language and, to a lesser extent, by their religion. The language persisted, because of the continual migration of families from North Wales throughout the nineteenth century and because of the central role of the chapel in the life of the community [42]. Like the Irish, the Welsh were employed in shipping and on the docks, although they were also important in the development of the local building industry [43].

In contrast, the Merseyside Scots did not on the whole speak a different language, although some would have been Gaelic speakers. And the Presbyterian church had many similarities to English non-conformist denominations. It could be argued that, as a result of the Scottish education system, many Scots were employed in medicine and the professions and many were commercial entrepreneurs. As a result, the Scots were not ghettoised and were perhaps not so obviously a migrant group as many others in the nineteenth century.

This would seem to be borne out by the fact that Scots did not tend to locate in identifiable parts of the city, as discussed in Chapter Two. On the other hand, the Scots do appear to have operated much more as a 'community' than the Irish, particularly through the various Caledonian societies in the area. Much has been written about such societies, particularly abroad, and they have been criticised for projecting an unreal view of their homeland. This is not perhaps a criticism which can be levelled at the Merseyside societies - at least not for most of their existence - as their membership contained many first generation Scots as migration continued right up to the Second World War. The founding of the Liverpool Scottish regiment may also be seen as a key element in the operation of the Scottish 'community' on Merseyside.

There is a stark contrast with the Irish here, as Irish clubs and societies are a relatively recent phenomenon. Indeed, Bernard Shaw opposed such establishments, arguing that if Irish people flocked together like geese, they might just as well have stayed in Ireland. There was little community leadership in the period before the Second World War and the Irish Club in London was only founded in 1947. Thus,

> the 'community' feeling among the million Irish-born who reside, for the most part, permanently in Britain is a comparatively recent development and certainly within the confines of the last decade [the 1960s]. They had, hitherto, been regarded as a community more by their hosts than by themselves [44].

Like the Scots, however, the Irish formed regiments in Britain such as the Irish Guards and the London Irish Rifles. They drew heavily on first and second generation Irish, consolidating a tradition of emigre service in the British army[45].

Finally, one further contrast between the Scots and the Irish on Merseyside is in relation to politics. Chapter Eight deals with the contribution of Scots to politics on Merseyside, many Scots having given service as Members of Parliament and as local councillors. Nationalist politics was not much in evidence, however, although there were small groupings of interested individuals within the Wallace Society and the Liverpool branch of the SNP. The concentrations of Irish families in tightly defined areas of Liverpool, on the other hand, enabled the Irish Question to be an election issue in the city. T.P. O'Connor, the first President of the Irish National League of Great Britain, was elected as the first and only Irish Nationalist candidate for an English constituency, when he won Liverpool Scotland in 1885, a seat he continued to represent until 1929. There was an attempt also to raise the Irish Question in 1922, in Exchange division, but without success[46]. Religious segregation within Liverpool was reflected in the presence of the Orange Order and of the Protestant Party, which was represented on the City Council in Liverpool until the 1970s.

Structure of the Book

The book begins, in Chapter Two, by examining the numbers of Scots migrants on Merseyside, in comparison, firstly with the other main migrant groups - the Irish and Welsh - and, secondly with other major English provincial cities. The pattern of settlement of the Scots on Merseyside is also examined. Although as described above, the Scots were less distinctive than the Irish in terms of their religion, nevertheless the Kirk played an important role in expatriate Scottish society and this is explored in Chapter Three. The chapter describes in detail the various Scots churches which have existed on Merseyside, at different times.

The various motivations behind migration have been discussed above. Many professionally qualified Scots brought their medical skills to England and the contribution of Scots on Merseyside to medicine is the focus of Chapter Four. Other Scots came south in search of commercial fortune and the Port of Liverpool with its developing trade with the Americas was a natural destination for migrant entrepreneurs. The role of the Scots in the port, in commerce, and in the development of many Merseyside shipping companies is described in Chapter Five.

Like the Irish, the Scots have an honourable record of service in the British Army and Chapter Six describes the history of the Liverpool Scottish regiment. Unlike the Irish, the Scots have always had an extensive network of social clubs and Caledonian Societies and the various societies which have existed on Merseyside are discussed in Chapter Seven. The chapter also refers to the charitable efforts of Scots over the years.

Chapter Eight examines the participation of Scots in politics on Merseyside, including those Scots who have represented Merseyside seats in Parliament as well as those active at a more local level. Finally, Chapter Nine seeks to draw some conclusions about the role of the Scots expatriate community on Merseyside, as well as looking in more detail at the position of that community in the 1990s.

One major area of Merseyside life in which Scots have made a significant contribution is football. The scale of the contribution is perhaps beyond the scope of this short book, although it should also be said that few of the footballers concerned were involved in the wider Scottish community in the area. For that reason, Appendix One simply lists those Scottish internationalists who played for Merseyside clubs, with some added commentary, where appropriate.

References   .

1. D. Baines (1985), Migration in a Mature Economy, Cambridge, p.10.
2. T.M. Devine (1992), 'Introduction: the Paradox of Scottish Emigration' in T.M. Devine (ed.), Scottish Emigration and Scottish Society, John Donald, Edinburgh, p.2.
3. R.A. Cage (1985), 'The Scots in England' in R.A. Cage (ed.), The Scots Abroad. Labour, Capital, Enterprise, 1750-1914, Croom Helm, London, pp. 29-45.
4. R.H. Campbell (1985), 'Scotland' in R.A. Cage (ed.), Ibid., pp.1-28.
5. I.D. Whyte (1991), 'Migration in early-modern Scotland and England' in C.G. Pooley and I.D. Whyte (eds.), Migrants, Emigrants and Immigrants. A Social History of Migration, Routledge, London, pp.87-105.
6. J.M. Brock (1992), 'The Importance of Emigration in Scottish Regional Population Movement, 1861-1911' in T.M. Devine (ed), Op. cit., pp.104-134
7. R. Dennis (1984), English Industrial Cities of the Nineteenth Century. A Social Geography, Cambridge, p.40.
8. C.G.Pooley and J. Doherty (1991), 'The Longitudinal Study of Migration. Welsh Migration to English Towns in the Nineteenth Century' in C.G.Pooley and I.D. Whyte (eds.), Op. cit., pp.143-173.

9. J.A. Jackson (1963), The Irish in Britain, Routledge and Kegan Paul, London.
10. V.G. Kiernan (1978), 'Britons Old and New' in C. Holmes (ed), Immigrants and Minorities in British Society, George Allen and Unwin, London, p.43.
11. R.H. Campbell (1985), Op. cit.
12. V.G. Kiernan (1978), Op. cit.
13. Ibid.
14. R.A.Cage (1985), Op. cit., p.32.
15. M. Brogden (1988), On the Mersey Beat, pp.7-11.
16. Ibid.
17. C. Holmes (1978), 'Introduction' in C. Holmes (ed), Immigrants and Minorities in British Society, George Allen and Unwin, London, p.18.
18. R. Lawton (1953), 'Genesis of Population' in W. Smith (ed), A Scientific Survey of Merseyside, Liverpool University Press, pp.120-131.
19. K.G. Pickett (1970), 'Migration in the Merseyside Area' in R. Lawton and C.M. Cunningham (eds.), Merseyside Social and Economic Studies, Longman, London, pp.108-148
20. R. Dennis (1984), English Industrial Cities of the Nineteenth Century. A Social Geography, Cambridge, chapter 7.
21. C.G.Pooley (1977), 'The Residential Segregation of Migrant Communities in mid-Victorian Liverpool', Transactions of the Institute of British Geographers, 2, pp.364-382.
22. J.A. Jackson (1963), The Irish in Britain, Routledge and Kegan Paul, London.
23. K. O'Connor (1972), The Irish in Britain, Sidgwick and Jackson, London.
24. P. Buckland and J. Belchem (eds) (1992), The Irish in British Labour History, University of Liverpool Institute of Irish Studies.
25. J. Bohstedt (1992), 'More than one Working Class: Protestant and Catholic Riots in Edwardian Liverpool' in J. Belchem (ed), Popular Politics, Riot and Labour, Liverpool University Press.
26. P.J. Waller (1981), Democracy and Sectarianism: A Political and Social History of Liverpool 1868-1939, Liverpool.
27. C.G.Pooley and J. Doherty (1991), 'The Longitudinal Study of Migration. Welsh Migration to English Towns in the Nineteenth Century' in C.G.Pooley and I.D. Whyte (eds.), Op. cit., pp.143-173.
28. T.A. Roberts (1986), "The Welsh influence on the building industry in Victorian Liverpool" in M. Doughty (ed.), Building the Industrial City, Leicester University Press, pp.106-149.
29. A. Murphy (1995), From the Empire to the Rialto: Racism and Reaction in Liverpool 1918-1948, Liver Press, Birkenhead.

30. I. Law and J. Henfey (1981), <u>A History of Race and Racism in Liverpool,</u>
    <u>1660-1950</u>, Merseyside Community Relations Council, Liverpool.
31. D. Frost (1995), 'West Africans, Black Scousers and the Colour Problem in
    interwar Liverpool' in J. Manley (ed.), <u>Black Presence in the North West,</u>
    North West Labour History Group, Salford, pp.50-57.
32. M. Christian (1995), 'Black Struggle for Historical Recognition in Liverpool'
    in J. Manley, <u>Ibid</u>, pp.58-66.
33. M.L. Wong (1989), <u>Chinese Liverpudlians</u>, Liver Press, Birkenhead.
34. I.L. Lynn (1982), <u>The Chinese Community in Liverpool. Their Unmet Needs</u>
    <u>with respect to Education, Social Welfare and Housing</u>, University of Liverpool.
35. G. Ben-Tovim et. al. (1986), <u>The Local Politics of Race</u>, Macmillan, London.
36. Commission for Racial Equality (1984), <u>Race and Housing in Liverpool: A</u>
    <u>research Report</u>, CRE, London.
37. R. Lawton and C.G.Pooley (1992), <u>Britain 1740-1950. An Historical</u>
    <u>Geography</u>, Edward Arnold, London, p.205.
38. A. Redford (1976), <u>Labour Migration in England, 1800-1850</u>, 3rd edition,
    Manchester U.P., p.137.
39. J.A. Jackson (1963), <u>The Irish in Britain</u>, Routledge and Kegan Paul, London,
    pp.86 and 88.
40. J.K. Walton (1987), <u>Lancashire. A Social History, 1558-1939</u>, Manchester
    University Press, p.183.
41. J.A. Jackson (1963), <u>Op. cit.</u>, p.127
42. T.A.Roberts (1986), "The Welsh influence on the building industry in Victorian
    Liverpool" in M. Doughty (ed.), <u>Building the Industrial City</u>, Leicester
    University Press, pp.106-149.
43. <u>Ibid.</u>
44. K. O'Connor (1972), <u>The Irish in Britain</u>, Sidgwick and Jackson, London,
    p.160.
45. <u>Ibid.</u>, p.54.
46. J.A. Jackson (1963), <u>Op. cit.</u>, pp.122 and 127.

The most typical image of Scotland is the Highland Games. A humble attempt to stage
the event in Liverpool in 1951 grew into a major annual event at Blackpool.
Pipe bands were a major attraction...

...the smartley dressed drum majors provinging a major attraction

In St John's Gardens is a statue of W.E. Gladstone, one of a Liverpool Scots family, who became Prime Minister. On the wall behind is a plague expressing the gratitude of the French Government to Liverpoletans (such as James Currie) for their assistance to French prisoners in the Napoleonic wars.

John Laird, whose statue stands in Hamilton Square, was Mayor of Birkenhead

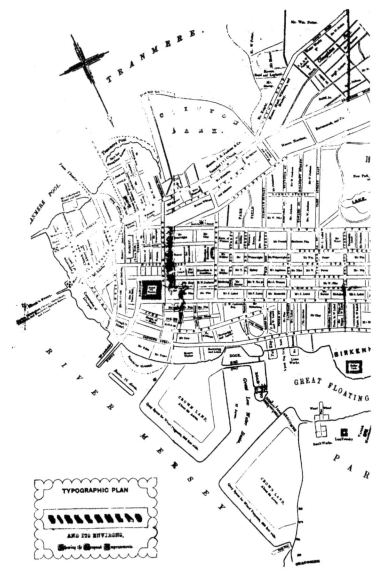

Law's Map of Birkenhead in 1844 shows the original site of Laird's Boiler Yard and Hamilton Square designed by Gillespie Graham. The "Scotch Church" is marked at the corner of Conway Street and Camden Street

CHAPTER TWO

The demography of
Scots on Merseyside

Introduction

The Census is the basic source of information on migration, allowing us to identify the place of birth of those persons enumerated; such data have been collected since 1851. That said, it must be admitted that there are sometimes drawbacks in using the Census. Concerns have been raised, for example, that the Census has sometimes undercounted and such undercounting is perhaps more likely in the case of migrant and minority groups, than in the case of a more settled population. There is too the fact that the Census **only** provides us with information on place of birth, as data on ethnic groupings were only collected for the first time in 1991. Thus, we are only in a position to study first generation migrants, from Scotland, Ireland or elsewhere. Second generation migrants, who may identify with their parents' culture, despite being born on Merseyside, can not be identified. Nevertheless, the Census remains an important data source and this chapter seeks to provide as much demographic information as possible on the Merseyside Scots.

Data from the Census

From 1851 onwards, the Census has collected data on the place of birth of those persons enumerated, and Table One and Table Two show the proportion of the population of both Liverpool and Birkenhead born in Scotland, in comparison with the Welsh and Irish, the other main migrant groups. The dominance of Irish migrants in mid-nineteenth century Liverpool is clearly evident, with the Scots a little way behind the Welsh as the third of the major migrant groups. The Scots are similarly in third position in Birkenhead but here, the Welsh are the most important migrant group from 1901 onwards. The Irish were never as completely dominant here as on the other side of the Mersey.

In terms of location **within** Liverpool, Pooley has undertaken detailed work on the 1871 Census and identified the main areas of settlement. The Irish core area was in north-central Liverpool, which was an area of mainly high-density, sub-standard housing. Many of the Irish here were unskilled, presumably obtaining some employment in the docks, There was also a second, mainly skilled working class group of Irish who were located more evenly across Liverpool, notably in the Everton district. Everton, which was then an area typified by medium-density terrace housing was also the main focus of Welsh settlement, while there were other smaller Welsh communities in central Liverpool and in the southern suburb of Toxteth Park.

The main concentration of Scots was to the north of the city in Kirkdale, a mainly working class area but ranging from poor quality housing near the docks to middle-status housing further east. The Scots therefore spanned a range of social areas in north Liverpool. There was, however, a separate cluster of high-status Scots in the Mount Pleasant and Princes Park areas [1].

Pooley suggests that the Scots in Liverpool did not group themselves into such an obvious 'ghetto' or 'ethnic community' as the Irish or Welsh which may reflect the range of occupations which they entered. Although the evidence is sparse, he indicates that the high status Scots in the south of the city were quite separate, both socially and spatially from the working-class Scots in the north.

Other reasons for the contrast with the Irish and Welsh may reflect social, religious and language differences. The Welsh, particularly those from parts of North Wales, are likely to have been Welsh-speaking, and Pooley suggests that the Welsh displayed a strong cultural coherence. Thus, very few marriages took place between a Welsh migrant and a non-Welsh spouse. This could be seen, argues Pooley, as either evidence of cultural insularity or as a positive action to preserve a Welsh identity in an alien environment. This was linked to Welsh religious institutions in the city and many churches conducted services in Welsh [2].

It is probable that language would also have been important for many of the Irish with a number of migrants likely to have been Gaelic speaking. Although some Scots would also have been Gaelic speakers, the majority would use English as a first language. Religion would have been of particular importance to many Irish, because they were mainly Roman Catholics, subsequently setting up their own churches and schools. Although the Scots had their own churches, they were Protestant ones and there was no separate schooling.

In comparison with the situation in other large English cities, the Scots community in Liverpool was a clearly significant one. Table Three shows the numbers and proportion of Scots-born in Liverpool and in the other northern cities of England from 1851 to 1991. The pattern this reveals is an interesting one. As might perhaps be expected, the proportion of Scots-born is greatest in Newcastle, the largest English city within easy reach of the Scottish border, but numerically, the Scots in Liverpool have been more significant, right up to 1931. In terms of Scots-born as a proportion of the total population, Liverpool was consistently in second place to Newcastle up to the Second World War.

The proportion of Scots-born in Liverpool was at its greatest in 1871, and this reflected a general increase in Scottish migration into England. The Census General Report commented that:

> The most remarkable feature.......is the decrease since the previous Census of people born in Ireland, the great increase of people of Scotch [sic] birth, and the still greater increase of people born in the colonies and in foreign countries [3].

The Scots in Liverpool, however, were at their most significant, in numeric terms, in 1881. The Census Report for that year devoted a part of its General Report to discussing Scots migration as follows:

> ..... of 1,000 natives of Scotland enumerated in England and Wales, 204 were enumerated in London or the closely adjoining town of West Ham, 94 in Liverpool or Birkenhead, 35 in Manchester or Salford, 46 in Newcastle-upon-Tyne or Gateshead, 19 in Sunderland, 12 in South Shields and 10 in Leeds, while in no other of the great towns was the proportion as high as 10 out of the 1,000 [4].

Thereafter, there was a steady downward trend in both the numbers and proportion of Scots-born, in Liverpool and elsewhere, through to the present day.

Patterns of Settlement

In 1901, the Census reports discussed the distribution of Scots-born as being a significant element within the overall enumeration of the population. The report stated that:

> The local distribution of persons of Scotch [sic] birth followed very closely the distribution of the Irish

and identified twelve counties with above average proportions of Scots. These were Surrey, Kent, Middlesex, Essex, London, Northumberland, Cumberland, Durham, Lancashire, Cheshire, Yorkshire and Hampshire. The report continued:

It is an interesting fact that these 12 counties are identical with those in which the largest numbers of Irish-born were enumerated; this preference of the Scotch and the Irish for identical counties or areas suggests that they are probably attracted thereto by similar considerations, viz., the greater certainty of gaining a livelihood in industrial and mining localities. Like the Irish, the Scotch are not attracted to the agricultural counties .....

In the large towns, excluding London, the largest number of persons of Scotch birth was enumerated in the City of Liverpool, where 16,998 were resident at the date of the Census, or 25 per 1,000 of the total population, as compared with 29 per 1,000 in 1891 [5].

The Census also identified that, during the 1891-1901 period, there was a trend of increasing numbers of Scots in both the London area and the north west, while the numbers of Irish-born were static or declining.

Table Three does suggest that, by the interwar period, the numbers of Scots-born were also declining, while the period after the Second World War shows a significant change in the pattern of settlement. From being the second most important northern destination for Scots emigrants (after Newcastle), Liverpool slipped to being the second least important with only Sheffield having a smaller proportion. By 1991, it was the least significant, perhaps reflecting the city's postwar manufacturing decline and an external image which suggested it was no longer a city which could offer adequate opportunities for Scots. It is perhaps no surprise that the relatively more prosperous Birmingham became numerically the most significant destination for Scots migrants.

It is important to recognise that Table Three is restricted, however, in that it refers only to the major northern cities. In 1921, the Census report did attempt to examine the proportions of Scots-born in all large towns, and identified eleven towns where the proportion was 2.0 per cent or more of the total population. Although Liverpool was not one of the eleven, the other three Merseyside county boroughs were. The Table (Table Four) was therefore dominated by the north east and north west of England. All four Merseyside county boroughs had significant proportions of Irish-born, and occupied four of the top five positions in the equivalent table.

In almost every case, the published Census reports provide us with details of the numbers of Scots-born but place of birth is rarely correlated with, for example, housing or occupation. In 1961, however, there was some occupation analysis for those born in the UK outside England and Wales (mainly this will include Scots and Northern Irish). Data are only available for the Merseyside conurbation as a whole but provide some useful insight into the employment of the Scots-born in Liverpool.

Table Five shows that while those born in the UK outside England and Wales represent 2.05 per cent of the total population, they represent a higher proportion of the economically active, as well as economically inactive adults. In terms of specific occupations, this grouping (mainly Scots and Northern Irish) follows a pattern broadly similar to the population as a whole but with some areas where there is a significant over- or under-representation. There is an over-representation in certain manufacturing industries such as gas and chemicals, engineering, woodworking as well as in mining, and, importantly in administrative and managerial posts. There is an under-representation in important industries like clothing, leather working, food and drink, and paper and printing, and also in clerical jobs.

Table One: Liverpool - Percentage of Scots, Irish and Welsh-Born

Year	Scots	Welsh	Irish
1851	3.6	4.9	22.3
1861	4.0	4.7	18.9
1871	4.1	4.3	15.6
1881	3.7	3.9	12.8
1891	2.9	3.4	9.1
1901	2.5	3.0	6.7
1911	1.9	2.5	4.6
1921	1.5	2.4	3.9
1931	1.2	1.8	2.5
1941	no census	-	-
1951	1.0	1.7	1.8
1961	0.9	1.5	1.6
1971	0.9	1.3	1.4
1981	0.8	1.0	1.1
1991	0.7	0.8	0.9

Birkenhead - Percentage of Scots, Irish and Welsh-Born

Year	Scots	Welsh	Irish
1851	n.a.	n.a.	n.a.
1861	4.9	7.1	14.4
1871	n.a.	n.a.	n.a.
1881	3.9	5.8	8.8
1891	3.3	5.6	6.2
1901	2.7	5.3	4.8
1911	2.7	4.5	3.7
1921	2.2	4.1	3.5
1931	1.7	4.0	2.1
1941	no census	-	-
1951	1.7	3.2	1.8
1961	1.4	2.5	1.7
1971	1.4	2.1	1.5
1981*	1.4	2.1	1.1
1991*	1.3	1.8	0.9

(* Wirral MDC)

25

Table Three: Proportion of Scots-Born in Selected English Cities 1851-1991

Year	Liverpool No. of Scots	% of pop	Newcastle No. of Scots	% of pop	Manchester No. of Scots	% of pop	Leeds No. of Scots	% of pop	Sheffield No. of Scots	% of pop	Birmingham No. of Scots	% of pop
1851	9,242	3.6	5,745	6.5	3,209	1.4	1,268	0.7	642	0.5	1,100	0.5
1861	17,870	4.0	4,981	4.6	7,971	1.7	1,402	0.7	1,060	0.6	1,432	0.5
1871	20,394	4.1	8,906	6.9	7,176	2.0	2,198	0.8	1,414	0.6	1,545	0.4
1881	20,434	3.7	8,732	6.0	6,089	1.8	2,654	0.9	1,594	0.6	1,667	0.4
1891	15,276	2.9	11,085	5.9	7,599	1.5	3,347	0.9	1,696	0.5	2,007	0.4
1901	16,998	2.5	12,031	5.7	7,515	1.4	3,911	0.9	2,213	0.6	2,335	0.4
1911	14,275	1.9	11,990	4.5	9,065	1.3	3,678	0.8	2,395	0.5	2,184	0.4
1921	12,301	1.5	10,278	3.7	8,239	1.1	3,873	0.8	2,643	0.5	4,809	0.5
1931	10,340	1.2	8,780	3.1	8,473	1.1	4,315	0.9	2,496	0.5	5,670	0.6
1941	no census		-		-		-		-		-	
1951	8,192	1.0	7,443	2.5	9,018	1.3	6,338	1.2	3,699	0.71	3,005	1.2
1961	6,700	0.9	6,096	2.3	8,756	1.3	6,813	1.3	3,794	0.81	3,139	1.2
1971	5,350	0.9	4,840	2.2	9,155	1.7	8,085	1.6	4,365	0.81	1,960	1.2
1981	3,951	0.8	5,672	2.1	7,571	1.71	1,193	1.6	4,214	0.81	1,422	1.1
1991	3,277	0.7	5,571	2.1	6,864	1.7	9,955	1.5	4,269	0.8	9,793	1.0

Table Four: Large Towns with the Greatest Proportion of Scots- and Irish-Born, 1921

	% per 10,000 persons	
	Male	Female
Scots		
Carlisle	706	748
Barrow	405	352
Newcastle	405	344
Tynemouth	329	262
Hornsey	253	224
Bootle	254	211
Gateshead	240	215
South Shields	249	204
Birkenhead	237	212
Wallasey	216	211
Hendon	199	207
[Liverpool	160	147]
Irish		
Bootle	656	501
Liverpool	410	371
Barrow	392	319
Birkenhead	359	344
Wallasey	287	300

Table Five: Merseyside Conurbation 1961 - Occupations of those in UK, outside England and Wales

Occupation		No. born outside England and Wales within UK	% of total population
Total resident		28,440	2.05
Econ. Inactive, aged 15+		10,980	2.83
Total econ. Active		14,830	2.32
I	Farmers, fishermen	130	2.66
II	Mining	40	4.40
III	Gas, coke, chemicals	240	3.32
IV	Glass, ceramics	30	2.14
V	Foundries, rolling mills	60	2.26
VI	Electrical workers	260	1.65
VII	Engineering workers	1,790	2.79
VIII	Woodworkers	220	2.78
IX	Leather workers	20	1.32
X	Textile workers	50	2.66
XI	Clothing workers	150	1.36
XII	Food, drink, tobacco	300	1.77
XIII	Paper, printing	170	1.82
XIV	Other manufacturing	230	2.22
XV	Construction	310	2.19
XVI	Painters, decorators	80	0.85
XVII	Drivers of cranes etc	230	2.53
XVIII	Labourers	1030	2.23
XIX	Transport, communications	1340	2.03
XX	Warehousemen, storekeepers	600	2.03
XXI	Clerical1	710	1.82
XXII	Sales workers	1320	2.10
XXIII	Services, sports and recreation	2050	2.83
XXIV	Administrative and managerial	500	3.57
XXV	Professional, technical	1610	3.34
XXVI	Armed forces	30	2.17
XXVII	Other	330	2.82

Conclusion

The material from the Census shows that, at certain times, Merseyside has been a significant destination for Scots, as indeed for other migrants, and from the nineteenth century through to the interwar period, there has been a significant Scots-born population. Since the Second World War, the situation has changed and Merseyside seems no longer to have a large number of Scots-born residents. Partly this may be due to declining opportunities in the area, which may no longer be seen as an attractive destination.

It is important to note that the Census data refer only to those born in Scotland and data on second generation members of migrant families cannot be obtained. There is no doubt, however, that there is still a large community within Merseyside which still regards itself as being of Scottish heritage and this emerges quite strongly in some subsequent chapters, particularly in relation to the social life of the community. The next chapter looks at the role of the church in helping to define that community.

References

1. C. G. Pooley, (1977), 'The residential segregation of migrant communities in mid-Victorian Liverpool', Transactions of the Institute of British Geographers, pp 364-382.
2. Ibid.
3. Census of England and Wales (1873), 1871 Census: General Report Volume IV, HMSO, London, p.xxii.
4. Census of England and Wales (1883), 1881 Census: General Report Volume IV, HMSO; London.
5. Census of England and Wales, (1904), 1901 Census: General Report with Appendices, HMSO, London.

Scots often made a contribution to more than one aspect of Merseyside life.
T.S. Traill, a medic, founded the Royal Institution and was one of the founders
of the Liverpool Institute.

The Royal Institution associated with T.S. Traill

The Liverpool Institute

Another medic, James Currie, was deeply involved in radical politics
and wrote the first biography of Robert Burns

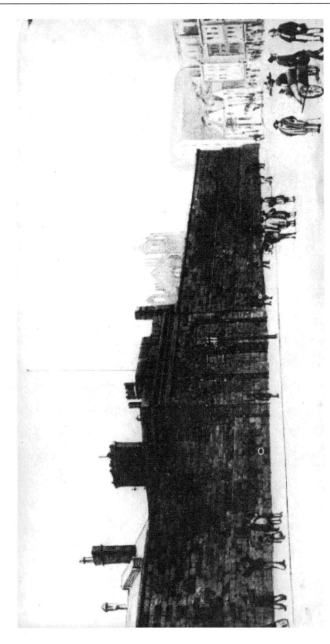

The conditions in which French prisoners of war were held in the Borough Gaol was the subject of one of his campaigns

CHAPTER THREE

The Kirk

Introduction

For many migrant groups, the church has a particularly important role to play in helping to preserve a form of community identity. In postwar Britain, the influx of people from India, Pakistan, Bangladesh and many African and Asian countries has been accompanied by the construction of mosques and temples which have become major community foci and many groups are located around such places of worship. Earlier migrant groups like the Irish, discussed in Chapter One, could also be characterised in most cases by a separate religious belief - in this case Roman Catholicism - and the Irish population on Merseyside, as elsewhere, became focused in particular parts of the city, served by separate churches and schools.

It should be noted, however, that geographical propinquity has not always been necessary for communities to operate successfully. The Armenians in London, for example, are highly dispersed across the city yet it is precisely for this reason that their community institutions and churches are so important in retaining an Armenian identity and providing a focus for meeting and for social interaction [1]. Pooley [2] has already showed how the Scots in Liverpool are not as geographically concentrated as the Irish or the Welsh; this suggests that Scottish community groups and churches have a key role to play in drawing together Scots from across the city. This particular chapter focuses on the role of the church.

Although the Scots, unlike the majority of Irish families, were Protestants, they also retained their distinctive Church adherence in their expatriate communities. Donnachie, writing of Scots in Australia for example, refers to 'education, culture and the Kirk - those three great manifestations of Scottishness overseas' [3]. In a more detailed study of Scots in America, Donaldson discusses the ways in which Scots, while having a great gift of assimilation, nevertheless carefully fostered and sometimes exaggerated, what they could preserve of Scottish life and Scottish ways.

> Not least significant was the retention of many of the characteristics of Scottish church life. The rigid discipline of the Presbyterian system was maintained in the United States at least as long as it lasted at home. Antiquated customs in worship survived........In America, as in Scotland, church services were provided in Gaelic for highland congregations [4].

Scottish church history is characterised by a significant number of schisms, often caused by disputes over the appointment of ministers and the powers of the congregations. The most significant split occurred in 1843, when two-fifths of the Church of Scotland's ministers walked out of the General Assembly, led by Thomas Chalmers, and established a Free Church. The bulk of this church was reunited with the Church of Scotland in 1929, although splinter groups remained as the United Free Church and the Free Presbyterian Church [5]. As Donaldson has pointed out,

> the Scottish genius for schism went overseas with the emigrants, and several of the Presbyterian secessions were perpetuated there........Not only were Scottish schisms reproduced in America, but Scottish emigrants even established sects unknown at home [6].

It is therefore only to be expected that Scots migrants on Merseyside would similarly seek to establish Presbyterian churches and, indeed, for the schisms within Presbyterianism to be reflected there.

Presbyterianism in Liverpool

For three centuries after the Reformation, Presbyterianism in England was dominated by Scots, who founded many churches and, until a Presbyterian college was set up in England in the mid-nineteenth century, provided most of the ministers. The first Scots Presbyterian meeting house in England was established in Horningsham, Wiltshire, in 1566 [7] so it was hardly surprising that the 12th Earl of Derby, speaking at a St. Andrew's dinner in 1792, commented on the lack of a Scots kirk in Liverpool. This stimulated a number of Scots living in the city to form a society to fund the building of a church in Oldham Street. Six people attended the first meeting, but others, including Sir John Gladstone, father of the future Prime Minister, were soon persuaded to subscribe.

While awaiting the completion of the building, the congregation met first at the cockpit in Cockspur Street, off Vauxhall Road, and then in a large room in Church Lane, off Church Street. The Oldham Street kirk opened for worship in the summer of 1793, with Rev. William Kirkpatrick as its first minister [8]. In 1812 the Caledonian School was opened in Oldham Street as well, and by 1824 there were 170 boys and 90 girls on the school roll [9].

In keeping with the pattern of schisms and secessions within the Church of Scotland, it was perhaps inevitable that such a secession would occur in Liverpool. In 1808, a group broke away to establish a new chapel on the corner of Gloucester Street and Silver Street, also operating a Sunday School which, in 1824, had a total of 98 on the roll. The congregation moved to premises in Marble Street, Williamson Square, until a new building was completed on the corner of Great Orford Street and Mount Pleasant in 1826. This was associated at first with the Associate Burgher Synod, which originated in a secession of 1733, became part of the United Secession Church in 1820 and the United Presbyterian Church in 1847.

Music in worship was a major controversy amongst Presbyterians and its use in services at Mount Pleasant was not to everyone's taste. The use of Watt's 'Hymns and Psalms' caused a group to break away in 1831 to worship in a room in Pilgrim Street and then in Russell Street, where all music save the 'Psalms of David' was rigidly excluded. This congregation survived only nine years, being dissolved in 1840. During this period, Rev. Samuel Spence from Dumfries was the only minister [10].

A further dispute in the Oldham Street kirk over the appointment of Mr. William M'Ivor as minister resulted in the group inviting Rev. Dr. David Thom (one of the unsuccessful candidates and recently appointed minister of Ardoch, Perthshire) to lead a new congregation. Like Oldham Street, it was to be strictly connected with the established Church of Scotland. The new congregation met in the Music Hall, Bold Street, from 23 March 1823 until the opening of St. Andrew's Church, Rodney Street, on 3 December 1824.

Designed by John Foster Junior, this was a very fine building indeed, with two short towers flanking a three bay loggia with fluted Ionic columns. Inside, three galleries were supported on thin columns and these in turn supported thin columns up to the roof. In 1872, a Sunday school was built in the grounds, in a similar classical style. The churchyard with its plain headstones, contrasting with the crosses common in Anglican churchyards, provides a Scottish atmosphere and a monument to a railway contractor, William Mackenzie, is a well-known local landmark. This is a large granite pyramid erected in 1868 [11].

Even in the short period while the congregation was in Bold Street, there were bitter doctrinal disputes with Dr. Thom, which were settled by his agreeing to accept Rev. Andrew Wilson as a junior colleague, on the opening of the kirk in Rodney Street. In June 1825, Dr. Thom was charged before the Presbytery of Glasgow (which was responsible for the Rodney Street kirk) with nine accusations of 'Holding and propagating sentiments inconsistent with the Westminster Confession of faith'.

The charges were upheld and he was removed from Rodney Street, but continued to lead a group of his supporters back in the Music Hall in Bold Street, from October 1825 until the General Assembly of the Church of Scotland suspended him from office *sine die* in June 1828. His congregation then built a small chapel in Bold Street, moving to one on the corner of Crown Street and Brownlow Hill in 1851. This was known as the Berean Universalist Chapel and closed on the death of Dr. Thom in 1862 [12].

Churchgoers living in the north end of the city found it difficult to travel to Oldham Street or Rodney Street and began to meet first in a loft in Clayton Street, off Byrom Street, and then in Carpenters' Hall, Bond Street. The foundation stone for a permanent building in Scotland Road was laid on 28 March 1842 and the church, dedicated to St. Peter, was opened on 21 May 1843. In the early 1840s, this district consisted of cottages with gardens occupied mainly by businessmen, but was soon to change its character, as cheap high density houses were built to accommodate workers at the north docks and Irish immigrants fleeing from the 'Great Hunger' [13].

Secessions and Disputes in the Church

As a result of the Great Disruption in the established Church of Scotland in 1843, most Scots' churches in England severed their connections with it [14] and this was reflected in Liverpool by further secessions. On 6 August 1845, a chapel on the corner of Sugnall Street and Myrtle Street - dedicated to St. George - was established by a group from Rodney Street and in May of the following year, a very fine church was opened on the corner of Canning Street and Bedford Street by a group from the Oldham Street congregation, after a bitter legal battle. After the Disruption, the Rev. Joseph Welsh, the minister at Oldham Street, had allowed Free Church Ministers visiting Liverpool to speak there. It was argued by most of the congregation, however, that Oldham Street was to be used only in connection with the Established Church of Scotland. Vice-Chancellor Wigram concurred, and a group including Rev. Welsh formed a committee to proceed with the erection of a new church. At first, they met in the Seamen's Church, Rathbone Street, until the Canning Street church was complete. The church formed part of the then newly formed Free Church of Scotland - known south of the border as the Presbyterian Church in England.

Most of the congregation at St. Peter's supported the Free Church cause, which gave rise to a legal dispute over the title to the land which had been acquired from Lord Derby for the established Church of Scotland, so the congregation moved to the Temperance Hall in Bond Street, and then to a fine new building in Great Oxford Street (later renamed Silvester Street). The church in Scotland Road was sold to the Liverpool and Bury Railway; they gave it to the Church of England to replace St Matthew's parish church, which had been demolished to make room for the railway, and it was rededicated to St. Matthew [15].

Two other churches should be mentioned at this point. A congregation of 'Covenanters' (or 'Cameronians') who had never accepted the Restoration settlement, had existed in Liverpool since about 1823, [See Note Five at the end of this Chapter], meeting first in Gloucester Street, then Russell Street, Sir Thomas

Buildings in Great Crosshall Street, Lord Nelson Street, the Brunswick Rooms in Hunter Street, Hackins Hey, and finally building the Reformed Presbyterian Church in Shaw Street in 1860. A dispute over the title deeds led to a breakaway group joining the Western Irish Reformed Presbyterian Synod and, eventually, establishing their own church in Hall Lane, Low Hill. The church in Shaw Street was to join with other churches in forming the Presbyterian Church of England in 1876, while the Hall Lane church always remained independent [16]. The other church was not a Scots' kirk, but was formed around 1846 by Irish Presbyterians who had previously attended one or other of the Scots churches, before establishing their own church in Upper Islington.

'The Porcupine', a satirical Liverpool periodical, described a visit to St. George's, the Myrtle Street church established in 1845, and reported favourably. The Scots who attended were apparently more generous with their 'bawbees' than the congregations of most English churches. The preacher, Mr. Grossart, was a fluent speaker who avoided euphemisms like 'the Evil One' or 'untruths', preferring to speak bluntly of 'the Devil' and 'lies'. There was an obvious desire to welcome and accommodate strangers - in contrast to what 'The Porcupine' found in other Scots churches [17].

St. George's was the first Presbyterian Church in Liverpool to have an organ, an innovation which caused some members to leave and eventually set up the United Presbyterian Church in Derby Road, Bootle, in 1860. St. George's never really recovered from their loss. In 1856 the Synod of the Presbyterian Church in England declared that 'the introduction of instrumental music in public worship is not approved by this church'. Nevertheless, the following year St. George's (together with St. John's, Warrington) was allowed to continue to use their organs, since they were already installed. Finally, in 1870, resolutions against instrumental music were rescinded [18]. Meanwhile, an organ had been installed at St. Andrew's, Rodney Street, in October 1865 [19].

The Canning Street Church was described by 'The Porcupine' as the church where the 'well-to-do leading Caledonians of Liverpool' worshipped [20], but it was deeply involved in social work. While still at the Seaman's Church, a Presbyterian Young Men's Evangelical Association was formed on 17 August 1845 for the distribution of tracts among the poor of the town. It organised Sabbath schools in Bedford Street (later in Stanhope Street) and Jackson Street. In 1847 it engaged a teacher to teach reading to ragged children in the evenings, and the same year, the Sessions

Record noted its support for the work of The Young Men's Society as it was now known.(The word 'Evangelical' had tended to be used for all societies associated with the Free Church of Scotland). From 1853, the Society acquired the old Auction Mart in Harrington Street where it operated a day school. In 1858, a Wesleyan chapel in Heath Street (later renamed Hyslop Street) was purchased and recognised as a preaching station, being handed over to the Church by the Young Men's Society. Activities included Sunday services, meetings for religious instruction, entertainment (lectures, readings and music), a mothers meeting, evening school, a Band of Hope (and later Temperance Society) and a reading room which was open every evening. In 1883, George Johnson M.B, C.M. was appointed medical missionary at Hyslop Street. There was also a Moorfields mission in Hackins Hey which moved to Vauxhall Road in 1867[21]. This served the docks area immediately north of the city centre, an area of great poverty, which had been the subject of a detailed study in 1842[22].

Naturally, music was a controversial topic at Canning Street, being limited to the psalms and appended paraphrases of scripture, until 1872, when a vote to introduce hymns was carried by 117 to 66 votes with 7 abstentions. In general, the minority seems to have accepted the majority verdict and a hymn book was first used on 4 November. However, it was more than twenty years before an organ was deemed acceptable, one being finally installed on 28 October 1893[23].

Other Churches on Merseyside

As the population moved out to the suburbs, new churches were built. In 1855, Trinity Presbyterian Church opened in Belvedere Road, Princes Park, followed in 1862 by one in Everton Valley and in 1864, by Princes Road Presbyterian and Fairfield (Beech Street) Presbyterian Churches [24]. In 1865, Everton United Presbyterian Church opened at the corner of Queens Road and Breck Road, after the congregation had met temporarily in a schoolroom in Queens Road [25].

Meanwhile, Scots Presbyterian influence was also strong in the Wirral. In Birkenhead, the foundation stone of St. Andrew's Church in Conway Street was laid on 31 May 1839 and the church was opened on 26 August the following year. Originally this was a church 'in connection with the Church of Scotland' but soon joined the United Presbyterian Church [26]. There was a church school - St. Andrew's Higher Grade Presbyterian School - adjacent to it [27].

'Annals of Liverpool' refers to a Scotch Secession church being opened in Grange Lane (later Grange Road) on 21 April 1848, with help from the Myrtle Street congregation, although K. Macleod Black speaks of it as opening in 1837 and being revived in 1846[28]. More churches were built as the population moved away from the centre of Birkenhead. In 1857, the Lancashire Presbytery of the United Presbyterian Church received a petition for a second church in Birkenhead and the foundation stone for St. Paul's church was laid in Church Road, Higher Tranmere in 1859, the congregation meeting meanwhile in the Craven Rooms[29]. In Egremont (Wallasey), a congregation began to meet in temporary premises in May 1859 until their new building, Trinity Presbyterian Church, was opened on 6 July 1863. And in May of the same year, twenty members from Grange Road began to meet in Claughton until their new church, also called Trinity Presbyterian, in Alton Road, was complete[30].

Trinity Presbyterian Church, Egremont was also heavily involved in social work at its Seacombe Mission from 1859. In 'Seacombe Presbyterian Church 1862 - 1937', the inhabitants of Seacombe in the late nineteenth century are described as 'mostly of a rough illiterate type'[31]. To uplift them, a disused Wesleyan chapel in Wheatland Lane (opposite Harlech Street) was acquired for a very full programme of activities including tract and Bible distribution, a Sunday school, temperance work, a mother's meeting and a sewing class ('to induce habits of industry and thrift among young women', as 'the young women of Seacombe had many temptations' and it was 'intended to help them meet these'.) There was also a youths' fife and drum band, a day school from April 1863, adult evening classes, a reading and recreation room, sunday services, household weekly prayer meetings and a penny savings bank[32].

A momentous event of national importance occurred on 13 June 1876 in the Philharmonic Hall, Liverpool, (adjacent to St. George's, Myrtle Street) when the English congregations of the United Presbyterian Church and the Free Church of Scotland met to form the Presbyterian Church of England, after which it was difficult to identify churches as specifically 'Scots kirks', apart from those in connection with the established Church of Scotland, which formed its own Scottish Synod in England in 1851[33]. Scots did continue to play a prominent part in establishing further Presbyterian churches in the suburbs and in 1906, K. Macleod Black commented that 'Liverpool shares with Newcastle the honour of being the most Presbyterian town in the north of England' and noted that 'many English Presbyterian ministers are Scots'[34].

St. Andrew's, Rodney Street, in recent years

It took some time for St. Andrew's, Rodney Street, to recover from the loss of members to St. George's but its fortunes were revived during the ministry of Rev. James Hamilton (1894 - 1935). Quarterly Gaelic services, addressed by invited Highland ministers were well attended[35] and in 1907, Oldham Street kirk closed and its congregation was welcomed to St. Andrew's. Indeed, it is amazing that two kirks of the Church of Scotland, less than a quarter of a mile apart, had survived for so long.

The interwar period at St. Andrew's was unspectacular as the disputes of the last century had subsided and the long ministry of Rev. James Hamilton brought a period of stability. This was used to establish good relations with other denominations, especially with the Presbyterian Church of England, with whose ministers he frequently exchanged pulpits. Hamilton was well known in Liverpool and in 1926-27, he held the prestigious office of President of the Athenaeum. After his death on 24 February 1935, he was succeeded by Rev. David Douglas, who died tragically on 23 June 1937. During his short ministry, Douglas lived, interestingly, at the former home of the Gladstones at 62 Rodney Street.

After the Second World War, St. Andrew's experienced considerable decline, its smaller congregation no doubt reflecting the declining number of Scots on Merseyside. The church itself began to fall into disrepair and, by 1975, the congregation began to look for alternative premises. It had been hoped to demolish the existing church, while retaining one tower, and to build another smaller church and some office buildings on the site, but the church's listed building status prevented demolition. As an alternative, the congregation explored the possibility of selling the building to the Everyman Theatre, for use for theatrical purposes[36], but this plan failed to come to fruition. On 5 November 1983, the building was severely damaged by fire and has stood derelict ever since; one of its distinctive towers has in fact been demolished[37].

The building was sold off in 1988 and various planning applications were granted, including office use and a surgery, although none seems to have been financially viable. In 1994, Liverpool John Moores University, which owns much of the surrounding property, expressed interest in acquiring it as a central reception point and a symbolic gateway for its rather scattered campus.

Meanwhile, the St. Andrew's congregation itself has, since 1975, used the Western Rooms of the Anglican Cathedral (at the other end of Rodney Street) for Sunday worship.

Conclusion

It can be seen that the Presbyterian presence on Merseyside was of some significance in the nineteenth and early twentieth centuries and that the kirks which were established were important in preserving a sense of 'Scottishness' within the expatriate community in the area. As far as the Presbyterian Church itself was concerned, the state of the Church in Scotland was closely mirrored by the various secessions and new churches established within Liverpool and the Wirral.

There is no doubt, however, that Presbyterianism is now relatively insignificant within Merseyside. At the time of writing, the English Presbyterians have merged with the Congregationalists to form the United Reformed Church and while there remains a small Church of Scotland congregation within Liverpool, it no longer has its own premises. The future of its former building, St. Andrew's Church in Rodney Street, remains very much in doubt. As Scottish immigration into Merseyside has reduced, there are fewer new members joining the congregation; as it ages, it is hard to believe that it can be sustained in the longer term.

References

1. V. Talai (1989), Armenians in London. The management of social boundaries, Manchester University Press, Manchester.
2. C. G. Pooley (1977), 'The residential segregation of migrant communities in mid-Victorian Liverpool', Transactions of the Institute of British Geographers 2, pp.364-382.
3. I. Donnachie (1992), 'The Making of "Scots on the Make": Scottish Settlement and Enterprise in Australia, 1830-1900' in T. M. Devine (ed.), Scottish Emigration and Scottish Society, John Donald, Edinburgh, pp.135-153.
4. G. Donaldson (1966), The Scots Overseas, Robert Hale, London, pp.124-125.
5. T. C. Smout (1986), A Century of the Scottish People, 1830-1950, Collins, London, ch.8.
6. G. Donaldson (1966), Op.cit., p.125.

7. K. Macleod Black, (1906), Scots Churches in England, p.36.
8. Dr. D. Thom, (1854), 'Scots Churches in Liverpool', Proceedings of the Historical Society of Lancashire and Cheshire. Much of the information up to 1854 is based on this article. Although much controversy surrounded Dr. Thom, he writes in a very objective and factual manner without attempting to justify his own views.
9. Gore's Directories of Liverpool e.g.1864.
10. Ian Donnachie and George Hewitt (1989), A Companion to Scottish History, p.178.
11. Black, (1906), Op. cit., p.324.; Canning Street Presbyterian Church, 1846-1896, (1896), p.111.
12. N. Pevsner, (1969) The Buildings of England: South Lancashire, p.180.
13. Gore's Directory of Liverpool, 1859.
14. Canning Street Church (op. cit.), p.116.
15. Black, (1906), Op. cit., p.35.
16. Canning Street Church (op. cit.), p.116.
17. Ibid, p.114; Donnachie and Hewitt, Op. cit., p.178; Black, (1906), Op. cit., p.361.
18. The Porcupine, 5 May 1878.
19. Canning Street Church (op. cit.), p.121.
20. Black, (1906), Op. cit., p.312.
21. Canning Street Church (op. cit.), p.23.
22. John Finch, (1842), Statistics of Vauxhall Ward
23. Canning Street Church (op. cit), pp.13, 14 and 20.
24. Black, (1906), Op. cit., pp.55-57; Gore's Directories
25. The Porcupine, 29 March 1873. (Black gives 1861 as the date of opening of Everton U.P. Church. There are several discrepancies, between various sources, on the opening dates of various churches. This may be because temporary premises were used by some churches before they were complete or because some were recognised only as 'preaching stations' rather than churches, at first.
26. Gore's Directory, 1859.
27. Gore's Directory, 1895.
28. Black, (1906), Op. cit., pp.9-11.
29. Ibid, p.341.
30. Ibid, p.361.
31. Seacombe Presbyterian Church (1937), p.11.
32. Ibid, pp.18-26.

33. Black, (1906), Op. cit., pp.22-23.
34. Ibid, p.338.
35. Black, (1906), Op. cit., p.29.
36. Liverpool Echo, 4 August 1975.
37. St. Andrew's Kirk, Rodney Street, (notes printed by the church)

St Andrew's Church. Cockspur Street

Oldham Street Church

Note One

K. Macleod Black lists nine Scots' kirks which existed in Liverpool. These are as follows:

Oldham Street	1803	Church of Scotland
Rodney Street	1823	" "
Mount Pleasant	1828	Associate Burgher United Reform.
Russell Street	1831	United Secession (now extinct)
Canning Street	1844	Free Church of Scotland
Myrtle Street	1845	" " "
Shaw Street	1860	Cameronian
Queens Road	1861	United Presbyterian
Princes Road	1864	" "

He omits St. Peter's, Silvester Street. (which was certainly still in existence when he published his book) and the Berean Universalist Chapel

Gore's Directory for 1875 (the eve of the formation of the Presbyterian Church of England) lists several other churches which were certainly associated with the Free Church of Scotland (including the 'Irish Church' in Islington, Belvedere Road and Fairfield) and the United Presbyterian Church (including Derby Road and Vauxhall Road).

Note Two

One of the preachers at the opening of St. Andrew's, Rodney Street, was Rev. Edward Irving, who left the Church of Scotland to become one of the leading theologians of a new sect - the Catholic Apostolic Church. It was ultra-Catholic in ritual and liturgy, and ultra-pentecostal in its uses of speaking in tongues and prophecy. Twelve new apostles were appointed and the Second Coming was expected in their lifetime. When the last one died in 1901, the Church lost credibility. It did, however, give Liverpool a very fine church building in Catherine Street, which today, like St. Andrew's, Rodney Street, is standing in ruins.

Note Three

The Music Hall referred to in Bold Street was not the fine building which still exists as a booksellers on the corner of Concert Street. This in fact replaced the simpler building which was used as temporary premises for two Scots congregations.

Note Four

Canning Street church was sold to the German Evangelical Church in 1931 and demolished in 1952.

Note Five

The Cameronians trace their origin to the Covenanters who opposed the restoration of Episcopalianism as the established faith throughout Britain under Charles II and James VII (II of England). They set up illegal churches ('conventicles'), which were often put down with great brutality. They took their name from a preacher, Richard Cameron, who was killed by dragoons and they were heavily defeated at the Battle of Bothwell Bridge in 1679. Nevertheless, their opposition to state interference in the Church continued, even after the Revolution Settlement of 1690 (under William III) restored Presbyterianism to Scotland. After 1743, they became officially known as the Reformed Presbyterian Church.

This map appeared in K. Macleod Black's "Scots Churches in England" in 1906. It is probably not completely accurate but does illustrate the concentration of churches in the Londens area, the North of England and Lancashire and Cheshire

St. Andrew's, Rodney Street in the nineteenth century

The ruins of St Andrew's Church, Rodney Street

The Sunday School in the grounds of St. Andrews, Rodney Street

The Pyramid in the grounds of St Andrews, Rodney Street

The original Music Hall in Bold Street where the congregation of St Andrew's
Church of Scotland met (pending the completion of the Rodney Street Church
and to which a splinter group later returned)

Canning Street Presbyterian Church,

LIVERPOOL.

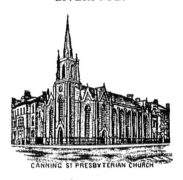

Ministers:

1846—1878.	1880—1896.
Rev. J R. WELSH, A.M.	*Rev. S. R. MACPHAIL, M.A.*

PROGRAMME

OF THE

Jubilee Celebration Gatherings,

3rd to 7th MAY, 1896.

Services.

Sunday, 3rd May, 1896.

Forenoon (at 10 a.m.) ...   **Address to Young Men and Maidens.**
REV. S. R. MACPHAIL, M.A.

„   (at 11 a.m.) ...   REV. PRINCIPAL RAINY, D.D.
Text—1 Cor. i., 22, 23, 24.

Afternoon ...   .   **Address to Young People.**
REV. WILLIAM HUTTON.
Text—Luke ii., 49.

Evening ...   .   REV. PRINCIPAL RAINY, D.D.
Text—Mark x., 14.

Precentor ...   ...   MR. G. T. LENTON.
Organist ...   ...   MR. JAMES NISBET, L.R.A.M.
Church Officer ...   MR. J. McKINLAY.

54

Musical Festival.

On *WEDNESDAY EVENING, 6th MAY, 1896.*

Chairman—ALEXANDER GUTHRIE, Esq.

CHORUS OF 100 VOICES.

Programme.

ADDRESS by THE CHAIRMAN.

TE DEUM LAUDAMUS (in F)	*H. Smart*
SOLO ... ... "With Verdure Clad" ... ... *Haydn*	
Miss MARY LANGDON.	
SOLO ... ... "In Native Worth" (Creation) ... ...*Haydn*	
Mr. J. WORK.	
RECIT. ... "In Splendour Bright" }(Creation) ...*Haydn*	
CHORUS ... "The Heavens are Telling" }	
SOLO ... ... "Why do the Nations" ... ...*Handel*	
Mr. G. T. LENTON.	
ANTHEM ... ..."O Give Thanks" ... ...*Henry Purcell*	
ORGAN SOLO ... "Sonata in B flat, No. 4" ... *Mendelssohn*	
Mr. H. A. BRANSCOMBE.	

COLLECTION.

ADDRESS by the Rev. J. K. NUTTALL.

CHORUS ..."We never will bow down" (Judas Maccabæus)...*Handel*

ORGAN SOLO ... ... "Offertoire in G" ... ... *Wély*
Mr. H. A. BRANSCOMBE.

CHORUS ..."How Lovely are the Messengers" (St. Paul) *Mendelssohn*

SOLO ... "I know that my Redeemer Liveth" (Messiah)...*Handel*
Miss MARY LANGDON.

CHORUS ... ... "Hallelujah!" (Messiah) ... ...*Handel*

DOXOLOGY.

Conductor—Mr. G. T. LENTON.   *Organist*—Mr. H. A. BRANSCOMBE.

55

Inscription on Memorial Tablet in the Church.

IN MEMORIAM.

THE

Rev. Joseph Rodger Welsh, A.M.

ORDAINED MINISTER
OF THE SCOTCH CHURCH, OLDHAM STREET, IN 1842,
HE LEFT IT IN 1844 WITH
MOST OF THE CONGREGATION, WHO THEN COMMENCED
THE BUILDING OF THIS CHURCH
WHICH WAS OPENED IN MAY, 1846.

HERE HE CONTINUED HIS FAITHFUL MINISTRY TILL THE DAY OF HIS DEATH,
WHICH TOOK PLACE VERY SUDDENLY
On 21st October, 1878.

ON THE PREVIOUS EVENING HE PREACHED FROM LUKE XII., 42, 43.
"AND THE LORD SAID, WHO THEN IS THAT FAITHFUL
AND WISE STEWARD WHOM HIS LORD
SHALL MAKE RULER OVER HIS HOUSEHOLD, TO GIVE THEM THEIR PORTION OF
MEAT IN DUE SEASON?

BLESSED IS THAT SERVANT WHOM HIS LORD WHEN HE COMETH
SHALL FIND SO DOING."

THUS HIS LORD FOUND HIM.

IN LOVING AND GRATEFUL REMEMBRANCE OF HIS LIFE AND WORK
MEMBERS OF HIS CONGREGATION ERECT THIS TABLET.

His body lies in Toxteth Park Cemetery.

Canning Street Presbyterian Church interior

Seamen's Church, Rathbone Street, the original meeting place of the Canning Street Kirk

Hyslop Street Medical Mission, operated by the canning Street Kirk

Canning Street Presbyterian Church

59

The interior of the old Philharmonic Hall, probably the venue for the first Burns Dinner
in Liverpool in 1859 and, more importantly, where a number of Scots secession
Churches met in 1876 to form the Presbyterian Church of England.

The exterior of the old Philharmonic Hall. St. George's Presbyterian Church
can be seen in the background.

Trinity Presbyterian Church in Alton Road, Oxton illustrates the magnificent architechture often associated with successful Scots communities in the suburbs.

The fine hall of Fairfield Presbyterian Church (dedicated to the memory of Rev. R.H. Lundie) still survives although the Church itself has been demolished.

CHAPTER FOUR

The Scots and Medicine

Introduction

One of the most significant contributions made by Scotland to British life in the late eighteenth and nineteenth centuries was in the field of education. Scotland had four universities at a time when England had only two, and Edinburgh University in particular seems to have had a high reputation. According to Smout,

> after the lawyers, the profession which contributed most to the life of eighteenth century Edinburgh was undoubtedly that of teacher.......The University reached the height of its reputation between 1760 and 1820......The Medical School of the University, founded in 1726, had immense prestige, due in no small measure to the professional dynasty of the Monros, three generations of whom, each called Alexander Monro, held the Chair of Anatomy in unbroken succession from 1720 to 1846[1].

In fact, although as Smout points out, the Universities of Edinburgh and Glasgow were the principal seminaries of doctors in the British Isles, their output of degrees was small. By the 1790s, Edinburgh was conferring only around forty medical degrees a year and most graduates left Scotland to practise[2].

Many of these doctors went to the northern English cities and Scots founded medical schools, infirmaries and hospitals in Liverpool, Manchester, Birmingham and Sheffield[3]. As far as Merseyside was concerned,

> Apart from the clergy and dissenting ministers, there were not many in late eighteenth-century Liverpool who had undergone any great degree of education. But the physicians of the town were an exception.......In the North of England many of the leading medical men were graduates of the Universities of Edinburgh and Glasgow and, as Liverpool grew, it attracted its share of émigré Scots[4].

Clearly therefore, the Scottish presence in medicine was significant on Merseyside, as in other English towns of the period and this represented a major contribution by Scots to Merseyside life. This chapter examines that contribution in detail.

The first Scots medics on Merseyside
When the Liverpool Infirmary opened on Shaw's Brow (now William Brown Street)

in 1749, its first three physicians were one Oxford and two Leyden graduates [5]. Medical and surgical studies at Oxford and Cambridge were then very theoretical, whereas Leyden and Edinburgh had a high reputation for their practical training, and, as noted above, Edinburgh physicians and surgeons were to become prominent in most British towns [6]. In Liverpool, Scots were not only prominent in the medical profession but Scots medics played a major part in all aspects of the town's life. The law at that time, of course, by placing severe restrictions on the dissection of corpses definitely hindered the teaching of anatomy and it is well known that Edinburgh achieved its pre-eminence, largely by breaking the law. Nevertheless, it is not surprising that the next two physicians to be appointed to the Liverpool Infirmary were Edinburgh graduates.

One of them was John Bostock, who made a very useful study of mortality rates in Liverpool. The other was Matthew Dobson, who did valuable work on the treatment of fever. Much of this work involved the use of a 'sweating room' and he was able to persuade his assistants to act as guinea pigs for his studies on the effects of excessive heat on body temperature and pulse rate. He published *A Medical Commentary on Fixed Air*, but was best known for his pioneering work on diabetes. He succeeded in isolating sugar from urine and established a test for the diagnosis of diabetes - basically by tasting the urine!

Dobson was the first Liverpool doctor to be elected a Fellow of the Royal Society (in 1778), the first President of the Liverpool Medical Library in the Infirmary (in 1779) and retired through ill-health in 1880 [7].

Dr. James Carson, who was also to become a Fellow of the Royal Society, qualified in Edinburgh in 1779 at the age of 28, after a change of career; he had previously been a Church of Scotland minister. His medical work was entirely in Liverpool. Almost immediately after arriving in the town, he became unpopular with its establishment, by appearing in court to give evidence for the defence of Charles Angus, who had been charged with murder. Carson's evidence resulted in the acquittal of the accused but contradicted that of a senior colleague and he was to remain an anti-establishment figure to the end.

Nevertheless, Carson did much valuable research. He admired William Harvey, whose work on the circulation of the blood was then undisputed but his research went much further. In 1799, he presented his doctoral thesis in Edinburgh on the subject *De Viribus Quibus Sanguis Circumvehitur*. Although it was accepted, Carson believed that some members of the Faculty had condemned it. He showed that the return of blood to the lungs was due partially to the action of the lungs and not only the heart, as Harvey believed, ideas which he developed in *An Inquiry into the Motion of the Blood*, which he published in 1815.

He studied lung collapse and carried out experiments on a recently slaughtered bullock in 1815. He believed that the constant movement of the lungs hindered the healing of pulmonary conditions but noticed that wounds from sabres and bullets tended to heal spontaneously, when associated with lung collapse and thought that the gradual collapse of the lungs could be beneficial in treating pulmonary diseases or abscesses. In 1822, he experimented successfully on animals but, in the same year, an attempt (by a colleague) to apply the principle to a patient suffering from tuberculosis was unsuccessful, as the patient died shortly afterwards. Seventy-three years later, his theoretical ideas were proved right, when the Italian, Forlanini, developed a successful technique for the collapse of the lungs in 1895.

In 1838, Carson found another application for his studies and patented a method of slaughtering animals by bilateral collapse of the lungs, which he thought would retain the lymphatic, lacteal and other fine juices of the body. But there is no evidence that this was actually put into practice.

Amongst the offices Carson held in Liverpool were physician to the workhouse, the fever hospital, and the asylum for the pauper lunatics and he was also in charge of the military hospital [8].

Dr. Carson was elected to the Borough Council for Abercromby Ward in 1835, and was appointed to a committee to 'promote the Improvement and Education of the Poorer Classes'. In April 1836, he suggested a seminary combining the features of 'a school and a university, except the granting of degrees', to be financed by shareholders with the Council exercising a controlling interest. The Council supported the principle of the scheme but was not prepared to commit itself financially. Dr. Carson then gave notice of a proposal to set up a committee to consider the 'best mode of establishing a University in Liverpool' for the Council meeting of 4 January 1837. This proposal, however, seems to have been withdrawn and his vision of a University was well in advance of its day [9].

Dr John McCulloch's practice as a surgeon and midwife was in Old Hall Street, adjacent to one of the poorest areas of the town and he had a sliding scale of charges, ranging from free treatment for the poorest to two guineas for the 'better class patient'. He left a useful record of the 4,832 deliveries he made between 1797 and 1820, giving details of the mother's name and address, sex of the child and fee charged; unfortunately he gave no clinical details. It was he who took the lead in establishing the first Scots' kirk in Oldham Street, described in Chapter Three.

His son, Samuel, went to Edinburgh, qualifying MRCS in 1812, and joined the army as a surgeon. After service in the Peninsular War and a posting to Canada, he returned to Liverpool, entered a partnership with his father and, like him, showed great concern for the poor, working as a surgeon at the Dispensary (for the poor), the Fever Hospital and the Workhouse Hospital. He died in 1853, his father surviving him by a few months [10].

The work of Dr. James Currie

One of the greatest names, both in medicine and in radical politics in Liverpool was Dr. James Currie, who was born in Kirkpatrick, Dumfries-shire in 1756. After working for a tobacco firm in Virginia, he returned to Scotland to qualify in Glasgow [11]. In 1780, he succeeded Dr. Dobson at the Infirmary. He campaigned successfully for the establishment of a lunatic asylum - he was amongst the first to see lunacy as an illness - and a fever hospital. He published studies on the treatment of fever with externally applied cold water and became a Member of the London Medical Society in 1788, a Fellow of the Royal College of Physicians of Edinburgh in 1791, and a Fellow of the Royal Society in 1792 [12].

Currie's interests extended well beyond his profession. He actively supported the establishment of the Botanic Gardens and the Athenaeum Library. He was a particular admirer of Robert Burns and on Burns's death in 1796, he organised a fund for his widow. In 1800, he wrote *The Works of Robert Burns* - the first biography of the poet to be published [13].

He made some enemies, particularly amongst the Tory establishment of the town. He was one of a group of radicals, mainly Unitarians and Presbyterians, who were known as the 'Liverpool Jacobins' and included William Roscoe (later MP for Liverpool) and the Rathbones. They formed a local branch of the Anti-Slavery Society - an act of considerable courage in a town whose prosperity was founded largely on the slave trade. Currie and Roscoe produced a pamphlet, *The Wrongs of*

Africa, and devoted the proceeds to the National Committee. They were in the forefront of the campaign for the repeal of the Corporation Act, Test Act and other discriminatory legislation against dissenters from the Restoration period. In 1790, Currie formed a local organisation. He published a letter in Gore's Liverpool Advertiser on 14 January 1790, and was one of four Liverpool representatives at a great dissenting meeting in Warrington, shortly afterwards.

The group were naturally sympathetic to the ideals of revolutionary France and totally opposed to the French wars. Currie put their views to the Prime Minister in a letter written under the pseudonym 'Jasper Wilson' - *A Letter Commercial and Political addressed to the Rt. Hon. William Pitt* - in 1793. The 'Liverpool Jacobins' were now so unpopular that Currie thought of emigrating to Virginia and actually borrowed £1,200 to buy a property there, writing 'the poor, persecuted and abused Presbyterians ....are preparing for emigration to America in vast numbers.' However, he was offered the command of a corps of volunteers, an offer which he declined, but he did agree to serve on a committee for the defence of Liverpool in the event of an invasion and for this work was eventually made a Freeman of the City in 1801.

This was not the end of his radical activities. By 1798, there were 4,000 French prisoners of war held in the recently built Borough Jail in Great Howard Street. Currie found them living in overcrowded conditions, with inadequate food and clothing and, when the French Government refused to contribute further to their wellbeing, enlisted the help of Mr. Roscoe and Mr. Rathbone to raise money to purchase food and supplies for them. This was not a popular cause at the time and the Government considered impeaching him for sedition, but his campaign did result in a Government Commission being appointed to visit the prison in 1801. In 1924, his efforts received some belated recognition, when he was honoured by representatives of the French Government, at a ceremony in St. John's Gardens, on the site of the old St. John's Churchyard, where 230 of the prisoners who died were buried [14].

This was not to be his last campaign. In 1802, his medical work led to a clash with the property owners over his views on cellar dwellings, then common in Liverpool [15]. There is no reason to believe that Currie ever suffered professionally as a result of his views and, as already stated, he was honoured by Liverpool in 1801. Finally, with his health failing, he retired to his native land but found its climate did nothing to improve his health. He died in Bath, in 1805 [16].

Dr. Traill and the Liverpool Institute

Another Scot, important in medical developments in Liverpool, was Dr. Thomas Stewart Traill, who was born in Kirkwall, Orkney, in 1781, graduating MD at Edinburgh in 1802. Indeed, it could be said that medical education and higher education generally owed its beginnings in Liverpool to him. It was he who suggested that Liverpool should have a Royal Institution, similar to that in London. It was to be expected that William Roscoe would support such a venture and the Institution opened in 1817, in a fine Georgian building (which is still standing) in Colquitt Street and received its Royal Charter in 1821. Traill became its Vice-President (Roscoe was President) and with the title 'Professor of Chemistry' lectured in that subject and was curator of its museum. Although the Dispensary in Church Street had given some medical education, the Royal Institution offered the first systematic courses, from 1834.

Traill wrote a number of articles on clinical chemistry and Liverpool became only the third provincial town to have its own medical journal, when Dr. Traill established the *Liverpool Medical Gazette and Monthly Journal of Medicine and Collateral Sciences*, which first appeared in January 1833 under the editorship of another Scot, Hunter Lane MD (Edinburgh 1830). It was not a financial success and ran to only five issues [17].

Dr. Traill was next inspired by the foundation of the London Mechanics' Institute by Dr. Birkbeck and it was announced, at a meeting of the proprietors of the Royal Institution, on 13th February 1825, that Dr. Traill had 'offered his services to assist and arrange the meetings of a Mechanics' Institute'. Dr. Traill addressed a public meeting in the Concert Hall, Bold Street, on 8th June and a subscription list was agreed upon. The Institute opened the same year and Dr. Traill gave one of the first courses - on chemistry. In 1827, he became the President.

In 1837, the Institute moved from its temporary premises into a new building, constructed in a classical style, in Mount Street. From it developed the School of Art (now part of Liverpool John Moores University) and two prestigious grammar schools - the Liverpool Institute High Schools for Boys and Girls respectively. Although the high schools closed in the 1980s as part of a local education authority reorganisation, they are still standing, and the boys' school has now reopened (through the energies of one of its old boys - Sir Paul McCartney), as a college of theatre arts. Herbert Tiffen, the official historian of the Liverpool Institute wrote that, although the schools had no single founder, 'it must never be forgotten that they owed their existence at first to the energy of Dr. Traill'.

Another Liverpool Scot who supported the Institute in its early days was Sir John Gladstone, who subscribed generously to it, and was its President in 1828 and 1829[18].

In his medical work, Dr. Traill was particularly concerned at the way in which restrictions on the use of corpses was hampering medical training, and the situation came into prominence in Liverpool in 1826, when the Master of the *Latona,* bound for Leith, opened three casks labelled 'Bitter Salts' which, after delivery to his vessel, had begun to give off a foul odour. The 'bitter salts' were found to be a preservative for eleven corpses. The carter who had delivered them stated that he had been hired by a man with a thick Scots accent and was able to direct police to number 8 Hope Street. The owner, Rev. James Macgowan said that he had let his cellar to a Mr. John Henderson of Greenock, whom he believed to be a cooper, exporting fish oil. The cellar was, however, found to contain 22 corpses. The police surgeon found no evidence of foul play and the bodies seemed to have been 'resurrected' from a nearby cemetery. It seems that the activities of 'body snatchers' in Scotland had resulted in better security in graveyards, so encouraging a trade in cadavers from England to the Scottish medical schools. Henderson was never caught, though others were, including one named Gillespie, who was discharged, and one Donaldson, who was fined £50 and sentenced to twelve months imprisonment. In November 1826, two men were caught delivering large boxes, found to contain cadavers, to coach offices in Dale Street, for dispatch to Edinburgh. The two men, John Ross and Peter M'Gregor, were each sentenced to twelve months imprisonment and a fine of £21[19]. The comparative leniency of the sentences suggests that there was some understanding of the situation which encouraged the trade.

Dr. Traill pointed out that more liberal laws in Ireland were attracting medical students to Dublin and away from England and Scotland. He gave evidence to the Select Committee on Anatomy in 1828 and this led to the Anatomy Act, 1832, which allowed a less restrictive use of cadavers in teaching.

In 1832, Dr. Traill returned to Edinburgh to the Chair of Medical Jurisprudence, where it was said that for the next thirty years, he never missed a single lecture[20].

Other important medics

Another Scots medic was David Waldie, who qualified in Edinburgh in 1831, where he knew James Simpson as a student. His main interest was in pharmacology and in 1839, he gave up his medical practice to become a chemist at Liverpool Apothecaries' Hall. When Simpson produced his first paper on the use of chloroform as an anaesthetic in 1847, he acknowledged that its use had been suggested to him by Dr. Waldie on a recent visit to Edinburgh [21]. In 1838, Waldie gave a paper to the Literary and Philosophical Society on the composition and manufacture of chloroform, stating that it had been used in solution as a medicine by a local doctor, Dr. Formby, some years before. This had led Waldie to suggest its possibilities to Simpson but Waldie's interest in chloroform was essentially that of a chemist and he made no claim to have played any part in its discovery as an anaesthetic beyond that [22].

A serious cholera epidemic in 1832 was to produce one of Liverpool's most famous Scots medics, Dr. William Duncan. Dr. Duncan was actually a second generation Scot, born in Liverpool, but his uncle was Dr.James Currie and he qualified as an MD in Edinburgh in 1829. He returned to practice in Rodney Street, Liverpool's 'Harley Street', as well as working for the Liverpool North Dispensary (for the destitute sick) in Vauxhall Road, one of the poorest districts of the town [23]. Like his famous uncle, he was never afraid of controversy and had his enemies in the town.

The cholera epidemic began in Russia in 1829 and was known to be spreading across Europe; many towns set up Boards of Health to prepare for its arrival in Britain. The Liverpool Board consisted of a few 'senior' doctors and a majority of laymen, much to the disgust of such anti-establishment figures as Dr. Carson, who vehemently condemned it at a public meeting. Nevertheless, one member of the Board was considered a leading authority on cholera. Dr. David Baird (MD, Edinburgh 1816) had been quarantine officer in Malta. On 18 January 1832, after the epidemic had arrived in Sunderland and was spreading through England, he lectured in the Medical Library. He had visited Newcastle, where the epidemic was serious, and expressed the view that it was caused by miasma - that is, infection spread through the air but exacerbated by unhygienic living conditions. This was quite controversial, as there was a strong school of thought which believed that the main cause was contagion, and disputes between the two views hampered preventative and curative measures. The epidemic reached Liverpool in April and Baird advocated removal of the unhygienic conditions which encouraged the disease, by a massive slum clearance programme which, it is perhaps unnecessary to say, was not carried out [24]. The Board's main response was the isolation of notified cases, which caused opposition - often violent - from crowds who still had a strong suspicion of the medical profession, after the 'bodysnatching' episodes described earlier. Many stated that 'in no cases....[are there to be]....anatomical examinations after death'.

In Liverpool, 4,912 cases were notified, with 1,523 deaths. This provides some indication of conditions in the town, especially when compared with the figures for Manchester - 1,267 cases, with 706 fatalities [25].

William Duncan's work in the Vauxhall area gave him first-hand knowledge of local conditions and he analysed the cases he personally attended in an article in the *Liverpool Medical Gazette* in 1833. Of 216 cases he described, 97 were living in court dwellings, 97 in cellars, and only 26 in houses. Only one seventh of the cases occurring amongst house dwellers were fatal, compared with a quarter of all the others [26]. He also contributed to a number of inquiries, namely the Inquiry into the Corporation of Liverpool 1833, the Inquiry into the State of the Irish Poor 1835, the Select Committee on the Health of Towns 1840, the Report on the Sanitary Condition of the Labouring Population of Great Britain 1842, and Inquiries into the State of Large Towns and Populous Districts in 1844 and 1845 [27]. There were Liverpudlians who felt that the problems of the town should not have been exposed to public scrutiny and Duncan was accused by a fellow medic, John Halton, of bringing notoriety to a 'good old town' but these Reports did result in the Liverpool Sanitary Act of 1846, with powers to appoint a Medical Officer of Health - the first in the country. Duncan was the obvious candidate for the post, not only because of his wide knowledge of local living conditions but also because he had studied medical jurisprudence at Edinburgh, the first university to teach it. A special committee appointed him to the post, part-time, at £500 per year.

Almost immediately, he was faced with a typhus epidemic in Vauxhall and the adjacent Scotland ward, aggravated by the vast increase in population and overcrowding caused by the influx of Irish immigrants fleeing from the 'Great Hunger'. His post was promptly made a full-time one, at £750 per year. Beginning from such a low base - Duncan described Liverpool as 'the unhealthiest town in England' - progress was sure though not spectacular. There were further cholera outbreaks in 1849 and 1854, which each showed a progressive decline in incidence and deaths; at one point the *Liverpool Mercury* accused him of murder, because he did not endorse a certain patent medicine as a cure for cholera.

One action which drew probably justifiable criticism was his determination to clear Liverpool's cellar dwellings. In this, as Thomas Burke said in *A Catholic History of Liverpool*, he 'blundered badly'. Though a laudable aim in itself, it was carried out without consideration for the availability of alternative accommodation. Many of those evicted were forced onto the streets or into already overcrowded lodging houses[28].

Today, Dr. Duncan is commemorated in the Duncan Building, the teaching block in the new Royal Liverpool University Hospital[29], and, until recently, in the 'Doctor Duncan's', a public house in Seel Street; this has, however - ironically enough - recently become an Irish theme pub! Dr. Duncan himself was actually born at the other end of Seel Street at number 23. Duncan Street in Liverpool, however, is named after Admiral Duncan.

The passing of the Anatomy Act 1832 encouraged the growth of medical schools. The Liverpool Royal Institution of Medicine and Surgery was formed in November 1834, moving to new buildings alongside the Infirmary in 1844 and changing its name to the Infirmary (later Royal Infirmary) Medical School. Incidentally, Dr. Duncan lectured there. This was the forerunner of University College Liverpool, which came into existence largely because of changes to the regulations for the London University external MB degree[30]. These developments ensured a regular supply of locally trained medics and so Scots became less dominant, although many continued to come south. One notable successor of Dr. Duncan was Professor Andrew Semple, who was Medical Officer of Health for many years after the Second World War.

Finally, there were other Scots who made significant contributions to medicine in Liverpool. They included John Cameron, who graduated M.D. in Glasgow in 1843, moving to Liverpool two years later. He lectured at the Infirmary School of Medicine and worked at the Southern Hospital, of which he was a major benefactor[31].

Sir William Mitchell Banks, M.D. (Edinburgh 1864) worked first in Glasgow before moving to Liverpool where he too taught at the Infirmary School of Medicine, becoming the first Professor of Anatomy and then Dean of the Faculty of Medicine in the Victoria University. He produced a number of research papers on hernia and cancer and received the honorary degree of LL.D at Edinburgh University[32]. In 1894, Banks was succeeded as Professor of Anatomy by A.M. Paterson, formerly Professor of Anatomy at Dundee. He held the Chair until his death in 1919. When

University College Liverpool began its programme of extension studies in 189, Paterson was a regular lecturer on 'Man's Place in Nature'. His great published work was *The Human Sternum* in 1904 [33].

Another Edinburgh graduate was Robert William MacKenna, a son of the manse from Dundee. He worked mainly in Liverpool, apart from service in the R.A.M.C. in the First World War. His main interest was in dermatology, on which he published a book in 1923. Like many other Scots medics, however, he had much broader interests and his writings also included a number of philosophical works and novels on Scottish life [34].

Liverpool did return one of its Scots to achieve greatness in his native land. Sir Donald MacAlister of Tarbert was born in Perth in 1854 but came to Liverpool and was educated at Liverpool Institute (Dr. Traill's 'foundation'). After achieving high academic honours at Cambridge, he was a lecturer and then professor at the Royal College of Physicians, President of the General Medical Council and, from 1904 to 1931, Principal of the University of Glasgow [35].

Conclusions

The high percentage of Scots doctors on Merseyside should not really be surprising. As has already been shown, this reflects the advanced medical teaching at the older Scottish universities in the late eighteenth and early nineteenth centuries. As Colley points out, in the century after 1750, Oxford and Cambridge produced only 500 medical doctors. Scotland, by contrast, educated 10,000. Many of these men naturally looked south of the border for employment [36].

Scots doctors were therefore active throughout England and Wales and not merely on Merseyside. That said, however, the particular conditions which prevailed in Liverpool in the early nineteenth century, in terms of disease, poverty and bad housing prompted a high level of intervention by the medical profession. The particular contributions of James Currie, Thomas Traill and William Duncan were significant in two ways. Firstly, they led to a greater awareness of the links between disease and poor living conditions, a controversial view at the time. Secondly, the establishment by Liverpool of the country's first Medical Officer of Health, and the founding of the Liverpool Institute provided lasting memorials to their work.

References

1. T.C.Smout (1969), A History of the Scottish People 1560-1830, Collins, Glasgow, p.353.
2. Ibid, p.256.
3. R.A.Cage (1985), 'The Scots in England' in R.A.Cage (ed.), The Scots Abroad. Labour, Capital, Enterprise, 1750-1914, Croom Helm, London, p.43.·.
4. S.G.Checkland (1952 -3), 'Economic Attitudes in Liverpool, 1793-1807', Economic History Review (Second Series), Vol.5, p.71.
5. J.A.Shepherd (1979), A History of the Liverpool Medical Institution, p.9.
6. Ibid, p.14.
7. Ibid, p.10.
8. (i) Ibid, pp.68-69.
   (ii) Lord Cohen of Birkenhead (1968), "William Harvey and James Carson FRS of Liverpool", Journal of College of Surgeons in Ireland, Vol 4, 1st July.
9. Thomas Kelly (1981), For the Advancement of Learning. University of Liverpool, 1881-1981, pp.26-28.
10. (i) Hist. L'pool Med. Inst., pp.21, 37, 62, 63.
    (ii) St. Andrew's Church, Rodney Street, (unpublished history)
11. Hist. L'pool Med. Inst., p.36.
12. Ibid, pp.64-66.
13. (i) Ibid, p.66.
    (ii) Ian Sellars (1969), "William Roscoe, the Roscoe Circle and Radical Politics in Liverpool, 1789-1807", Transactions of the Historic Society of Lancashire and Cheshire, 120, pp.45-62.
14. Hist. L'pool Med. Inst., pp.36-38.
15. Ian Sellars, Op. cit., pp.53-54.
16. Hist. L'pool Med. Inst., p.66.
17. (i) Ibid, pp.70-75.
    (ii) Thomas Kelly (1981), Op. cit., pp.24-26.
18. Herbert J. Tiffen (1935), A History of the Liverpool Institute Schools, pp.21-23, 129, 135.
19. Richard Whittington-Egan (1985), Tales of Liverpool Murder, Mayhem and Mystery, pp.15-20.
20. (i) Thomas Kelly, Op. cit., p.467.
    (ii) Hist. L'pool Med. Inst., pp.80-81.
21. Ibid, pp.70-71.

22. Ibid, p.126.
23. Eric Midwinter (1971), Old Liverpool, p.91.
24. Hist. L'pool Med Inst., p.84.
25. Eric Midwinter, Op. cit., p.85.
26. Ibid, pp.87 and 92.
27. Ibid, pp.86-87, 92.
28. Ibid, pp.96-97.
29. Thomas Kelly, Op. cit., p.408.
30. Ibid, pp.24-26.
31. Hist. L'pool Med. Inst., p.183.
32. Ibid, p.187.
33. Thomas Kelly, Op. cit., pp. 96, 103, 122 and 247.
34. Hist. L'pool Med. Inst., p.244
35. Herbert J. Tiffen, Op. cit., pp.163-164 and 129.
36. Linda Colley (1994), Britons. Forging the Nation 1707-1837, Pimlico, London, p.123

Bust of James Carson in Liverpool Medical Institution

The front page of Dr Carson's M.D. Thesis

Doctor Duncan

Dr Duncan's house in Rodney Street

Dr Duncan's name was commemorated in a public house in Seel Street

CHAPTER FIVE

The Port and Commerce

Introduction

Reference was made in Chapter One to the paradox of Scottish emigration - that
Scotland exported large numbers of its people, at the same time as the country was
industrialising and there were employment and financial opportunities at home. In
this sense, there are clear differences from Irish emigration where emigrants were
basically fleeing poverty and starvation. Yet, in fact, the two elements of Scottish
history are linked. Scots merchants had moved into the American trade in the
seventeenth and eighteenth centuries and Glasgow had begun to rival Liverpool
and Bristol as a point of entry for American and West Indian goods. Scots also had
a key role in the running of the East India Company, trading with the Far East: one
such individual, the Scot William Jardine, on leaving the company, established
Jardine, Matheson and Company which came to dominate the Chinese tea - and
opium - trades [1]. But such firms, while creating wealth for those involved, had only
limited impact on Scotland itself, other than as a vehicle for yet more Scots to go
overseas [2].

There is no doubt that Scottish entrepreneurship was significant. Sir Charles Dilke,
in his book *Greater Britain*, published in 1868, refers to the commercial success of
Scots emigrants:

> Whether it be that the Scotch emigrants are for the most part men of better
> education than those of other nationalities, of whose citizens only the
> poorest and most ignorant are known to emigrate, or whether the
> Scotchman owes his uniform success in every climate to his perseverance
> or his shrewdness, the fact remains, that wherever abroad you come across
> a Scotchman, you usually find him prosperous and respected.

> The Scotch emigrant is a man who leaves Scotland because he wishes to
> rise faster and higher than he can at home........[3].

Other, more recent authors have commented on the shrewdness and commercial
skills of the Scots and the significance of the overseas export of Scottish capital -
particularly to America but also to other colonies, such as Australia and India.

> ....upper- and middle-class Scots - though again difficult to quantify
> numerically - certainly brought capital, enthusiasm, entrepreneurial skills,
> hard work, and a determination to make good in their adopted country [4].

Scottish investment tended to be in three main areas, namely financial, shipping and industrial concerns. Such investment impacted not only on the adopted country but also on Scotland itself, not least in orders for ships from Clyde yards and orders from overseas markets for Scottish-produced goods[5].

The direction of Scottish investment in England is not always clear but it seems that there were particular connections with the north and west of England. Partly this was due to the increasing inter-relationship between Scottish and English industry, with labour beginning to move between companies on both sides of the border; partly the development of shipping and overseas trade, particularly in Glasgow, led to connections with related enterprises in cities like Liverpool and Bristol. All three ports were, after all, competing for their share of the American market. It is unsurprising then that there should be a Scottish connection in Liverpool's port and shipping industries. This is explored in this chapter.

Shipowners and Shipbuilders

One of Liverpool's pioneer shipowners was Sir John Gladstone, better known as the father of the future Prime Minister, William Ewart Gladstone; he came to Liverpool from Leith in 1784. He owned plantations in Guiana and, undoubtedly, owned slaves there, although it is not true - albeit often stated - that he was involved in the slave trade. He also had shipping interests and was responsible for much of the early development of Liverpool's trade with the Far East. He owned the *Kingsmill*, the first ship to trade directly from Liverpool with India in 1814, the year after the East India Company's monopoly of trade with India was ended[6] and, in 1835, the 449-ton *John O'Gaunt* was built for service as a tea clipper on the China run[7].

Sir John Gladstone was one of the founders of the first Scots' Kirk in Liverpool, in Oldham Street, his father having been minister of the North Kirk, in Leith. However, he became an Anglican and later founded St. Andrew's church in Renshaw Street, in 1815. This was demolished to make way for the Cheshire Lines Committee railway line into Central Station and the proceeds of the sale used to build St. Andrew's in Aigburth Road in 1893; this too is now demolished[8].

Gladstone was one of the benefactors of both the Liverpool Mechanics Institute (Dr. Traill's 'foundation', described in Chapter Four) and later of a similar (Anglican) establishment - the Liverpool Collegiate Institution - of which he was invited to become President. This was an offer which he declined in favour of Lord Francis Egerton, the second son of the Duke of Sutherland, but he was instead appointed Vice President for life[9].

One of the most influential Scots to be involved in shipping and commerce was William Laird, who came to Merseyside in 1810 to obtain orders for his family firm of ropemakers in Greenock. He settled in what was then a small village called Birkenhead and was to be largely responsible for its growth to a major port and industrial centre by the mid-century. In 1824, he was joined by his eldest son John (a solicitor) and they established the Birkenhead Ironworks at Beaufort Road, on the banks of Wallasey Pool. By 1828, they were pioneering the building of iron ships, and their first orders for iron vessels came from the Irish Steam Navigation Company for three lighters to work on the Shannon. In 1833, with John now in full control, Lairds also pioneered pre-fabricated shipbuilding techniques, supplying the City of Dublin Steam Packet Company with the *Lady Lansdowne* for service on the Shannon. This was shipped from Liverpool in parts and re-assembled on Lough Derg. Another innovation in the vessel was the use of watertight bulkheads.

By 1838, Lairds had built 17 ships, including the largest iron ship built by that date - the *Rainbow* - and the first screw driven vessel - the *Robert F. Stockton* [10]. As early as the 1820s, William Laird had plans for the development of docks to make Birkenhead a port independent of Liverpool and he, John Askew and Sir John Tobin acquired land along Wallasey Pool for this purpose. The Wallasey Pool was an ideal site, being a fairly narrow inlet, which could easily be controlled by a single set of dock gates. This was an inlet which provided deep water for over three kilometres inland, with soft alluvial deposits along its banks facilitating dock excavation. The Birkenhead Dock Company was formed and Morpeth and Egerton Docks were opened in 1847. The Company also expanded into Liverpool, purchasing the Herculaneum Dock, but ran into financial difficulty and was bought out by the Corporation of Liverpool. In 1857, two Acts, the Liverpool Dock Act and the Birkenhead Docks Act, vested all docks in Liverpool and Birkenhead (except for the London and North Western Railway dock at Garston) in the new Mersey Docks and Harbour Board [11]. Later dock extensions caused Lairds shipyard to move from their original site on Wallasey Pool to Tranmere beach (alongside the New Chester Road) in the late 1850s [12].

The older part of Birkenhead is laid out on a very well planned gridiron pattern, with some very fine buildings, and it owes this to William Laird and the Scot James

Gillespie Graham of Edinburgh, whom he employed to design the town. Near to the river was Hamilton Square, surrounded by stone faced buildings. Construction commenced in 1825, although it took some years to complete [13].

John's younger brother, MacGregor Laird, had a particular interest in developing trade with West Africa, which had declined since the abolition of the slave trade, and in 1832, with one Richard Lander, he led an expedition to the Niger Delta with three ships, one of which was the iron paddle steamer *Alburkah* built by Lairds. Most members of the expedition died of fever, but MacGregor survived and was able to report that the Niger Delta was navigable [14].

In 1852, he formed the African Steamship Company, with a fleet of small steamers built by Lairds. A charter was granted, giving the Company certain trading privileges, and a ten year mail contract was obtained. At first, they sailed from London but, from 1856, Liverpool became their base, with William and Hamilton Laird acting as agents in Liverpool with responsibility for the turn round of ships and their victualling, bunkering and repair.

After the death of Hamilton and MacGregor and the retirement of William Laird, the work was carried on by Messrs Fletcher and Parr. They in turn employed two young Scots, Alexander Elder and John Dempster, who were to play a major role in the continuing development of Liverpool's West African trade.

Alexander Elder was born in Glasgow in 1834. His father, David Elder, was manager of Robert Napier and Sons, engine and shipbuilders and his brother, John, was founder of Randolph, Elder and Company (later John Elder and Company and then Fairfield Shipbuilding and Engineering Company). Alexander left Fletcher and Parr in 1866, to become engineer and shipwright surveyor to the Liverpool branch of the Board of Trade.

John Dempster was born at Penpont, Thornhill, Dumfriesshire in 1837. His father, William, was the Duke of Buccleuch's builder and his business interests caused him to move to Birkenhead. In 1868, the British and African Steam Navigation Company was registered in Edinburgh and began to operate a service from Glasgow to West Africa calling at Liverpool, where an agent was required. Fletcher and Parr felt there would be a clash of interests in working for both companies involved in the West African trade and John Dempster was therefore invited to become the agent. His old colleague, Alexander Elder, joined him to form Elder Dempster and

Company. The service began in January 1869, with their first vessel, the S.S. *Bonny*, built on the Clyde by John Elder and Company.

After the first year, the two African shipping companies realised the destructiveness of their competition and agreed to share sailings. After Alexander Elder and John Dempster retired, the business was controlled by Alfred (later Sir Alfred) Jones - not a Scot but another colleague from Fletcher and Parr, and it was he who really built up the Elder Dempster empire, eventually obtaining control of the two shipping companies for which they had acted as agent [15].

Finally, Liverpool's trade with Spain owed much to William MacAndrew, who came from Elgin in 1770 and opened an office handling imported fruit. At first, small schooners brought fruit from Spain but in 1856, the iron screw steamer S.S. *Cervantes* was introduced to the run and by 1866, the MacAndrew Line was operating 34 steamers. The line remained independent well into the twentieth century, still specialising in the import of Spanish fruit [16].

The MacIvers

Undoubtedly the most dominant figure in Liverpool shipping at this time was Charles MacIver. The MacIvers were a Hebridean family, mainly from Uig in the Isle of Skye. In 1780, Iver MacIver set up as a merchant in Liverpool and was joined by his brothers, William and Peter. Another brother, John, was a shipmaster. In 1795, a group of Liverpool merchants, including the four MacIver brothers, purchased a former naval cutter brigantine, the *Swallow*, of which John became captain. On 12 February the following year, the *Swallow* was granted two letters of marque, authorising it to engage in privateering activities against French vessels and Dutch vessels respectively. The following January, these activities were extended to Spanish vessels. It is indicative of the MacIvers' standing that, in November 1797, they were engaged by the Government to carry the Governors of Bahamas and Barbados, with their families and servants, to San Domingo.

William MacIver and his partners were certainly involved in the slave trade. Records show that, on one occasion, the partners had transported 167 slaves to Savannah in the brig *Mars*. The family were Presbyterians and William, like Sir John Gladstone, was one of the founders of the Oldham Street Kirk.

In 1828, another of the family, David, came to Liverpool as agent for the Irish Sea ferry services of his father's firm, MacIver, McVicar and McCorquadale, who already operated coasters between Greenock and Liverpool. He saw the potential for a fast service between Liverpool and the Clyde (the West Coast railway route was not to be completed through to Glasgow for another two decades). He set up the firm of D. MacIver in Water Street and bought two vessels, the *City of Glasgow*, the fastest vessel in the world when first built, and the *John Wood*. In 1831, he was joined by his brother Charles, who had been working as a coffee and cotton merchant in Charleston, Carolina. On the death of his brother John in 1833, he inherited a fortune, which provided a sound financial base for the business. MacIver's soon realised that there was nothing to be gained from competition with their main rivals on the route, George and John Burns, and the two firms agreed to rationalise, with a joint service [17].

Good relations with the Burns family were to have a very long lasting benefit to the MacIvers. In 1839, Samuel Cunard, who was already carrying mail between the eastern seaboard of Canada, the USA and the West Indies, came to Britain with the aim of arousing interest in a transatlantic service. George Burns and Robert Napier (a Clydeside shipbuilder) were enthusiastic but it was felt that four vessels would be needed and so more capital was necessary. It is believed that MacIvers were reluctant to become involved at first but were persuaded to subscribe, by George Burns.

The British and North American Royal Mail Steam Packet Company was formed but, not surprisingly, was always referred to as "Mr.Cunard's Line". In fact, Samuel Cunard had returned to Canada, leaving the British operation in the hands of their agents, D. and C. MacIver, as the firm was now known. The service began, appropriately, on Independence Day 1840, with the first sailing by the *Britannia*. The other ships involved were the *Acadia, Caledonia* and *Columbia* - all wooden paddle steamers.

In 1847, the transatlantic service was operating weekly and the firm quickly expanded its services world-wide [18]. In 1864, *The Porcupine*, the satirical Liverpool periodical previously referred to suggested that the city was totally controlled by Charles MacIver:

> Look at the fleet of stately steamers - MacIver's American trade......the splendid fleet of screws - MacIver's Mediterranean trade......that glorious forest of masts - MacIver's Pacific trade......See yonder his Black Sea

fleet, his Baltic fleet, his Indian Ocean trade.......a majestic army - MacIver's
Volunteers.

The article went on to suggest that almost the whole town depended on him,
including postmen, whose work was mainly generated by him. It suggested that he
should be formally appointed dictator of Liverpool as he had

> a genius for dictatorship far beyond Cincinnatus, Julius Caesar, Thomas
> Aquinas, Cornelius Neipos or Michael Cassio.......One man in Liverpool,
> England or the World can alone save us from ruin. The trade is MacIver's,
> the town is MacIver's. Say but a word.....[and he]......withdraws his
> vessels [19].

Two references in the article require explanation. Firstly, screw propellers were
introduced to the Mediterranean service in 1852 [20]; secondly, MacIver raised and
financed the 3rd Battalion of the Liverpool Volunteer Artillery Regiment, with himself
as Lieutenant Colonel and Commanding Officer, and his relatives as Major and two
Captains [21]. The other ranks consisted entirely of artisans employed by the Cunard
Company [22].

Ships' stores for Cunard were supplied by the firm of Kenneth L. and Alfred Morison
(also Clydesiders settled in Liverpool). Charles MacIver married their sister Ann
and Kenneth left the family firm to become outside manager for Cunard, with
responsibility for the handling of their ships in dock.

Charles MacIver had long advocated the use of regular routeways across the North
Atlantic as a safety measure. With this, he had some posthumous success, as the
idea was taken up after his death and authority to organise it was given to Cunard [23].

Another shipping line which contributed to Liverpool's prosperity was the Glasgow-
based Anchor Line. In 1869, it inaugurated a service from Glasgow, through the
Suez Canal, calling at Liverpool, and for two years used ships loaned by Charles
MacIver, until they were needed for the expansion of MacIver's service to the
River Plate [24].

Coastal Shipping

As early as the sixteenth century, when Liverpool was just becoming prominent as the main port of north west England with the decline of the Dee, there was coastal trade with Scotland. Although Liverpool itself was a fishing port, Scots vessels were bringing in herrings to supplement local supplies [25]

A snapshot is provided by the diary of George Omond of Kirkwall, Orkney, who visited Liverpool in 1789. He and his uncle, John Reid, were joint owners of a vessel usually trading between Liverpool and Scandinavia and north Germany via Orkney. Their first vessel, the *Nancy* had been wrecked in 1787 and been replaced by the *Resolution*. Typical import cargoes included iron bars, timber and dried fish. Cheshire salt, presumably for preserving fish, was a major return cargo. Incidentally, George Omond was related to T.S.Traill, the founder of the Royal Institution [26].

Throughout the nineteenth and early twentieth century, there was considerable coastal shipping between Liverpool and Scotland, particularly the west coast. Gore's Directory for 1818 shows that packets operated regularly (although the frequency is not usually given) to Aberdeen (one vessel), Ayr (three vessels), Dumfries (three), Greenock (four, including sailings on Tuesdays and Fridays calling at Portpatrick), Leith (four) and Glasgow (sixteen).

Steam vessels were introduced to the route very rapidly and by the mid century, the trade had increased very considerably, although direct comparisons are difficult because the information given in Gore's Directories is not consistent. In 1851, the number of traders rather than vessels is given but there is more detail of frequencies. Two traders were sailing to Aberdeen, two to Annan (on Mondays and Thursdays), one to Ayr (weekly), two to Dumfries, two to Dundee regularly with another occasionally, one to the Galloway ports (twice weekly), one to Grangemouth (on Saturdays), two to Leith (one weekly and one on Wednesdays and Saturdays), two to Perth and five to Greenock and Glasgow [27].

It would not be appropriate here to attempt a full account of the coastal trade between Liverpool and Scotland but two companies merit special mention. There was a threat to mail after land communications with Scotland had been severed for six weeks by heavy snow in the late 1820s. Consequently, the Glasgow and Liverpool Royal Steam Packet Company (later M. Langlands and Sons Ltd.) was founded in

1836, with five ships to carry mail by sea. Three years later steam was introduced to the service when the *Royal Sovereign* began to provide a twice weekly service in each direction. Shortly afterwards it was joined by the *Royal George* and the frequency doubled. Langlands continued to expand its services until it was absorbed by Coast Lines in 1919 [28]. Another coastal shipping line dating from the same period was the Glasgow and Liverpool Shipping Company (later Robert Gilchrist and Company), formed in 1824. It had a fleet of fast schooners and, in 1862, moved its headquarters from Glasgow to Liverpool. It remained independent until 1943, when it too was acquired by Coast Lines [29].

Passenger traffic was important until the mid nineteenth century but the passage through the North Channel could be dangerous. On 18 June 1850, the paddle steamer *Orion*, carrying two hundred passengers from Liverpool to Glasgow ran aground and sank off Portpatrick, with sixty being drowned. They were buried in Portpatrick Old Churchyard[30].

Although through rail travel between Liverpool and Glasgow had been possible since the late 1840s, some passengers still chose to travel by sea. In 1910, G. and J. Burns operated a service between Glasgow (Broomielaw) and Liverpool daily (except Sundays) and Langlands operated cruises in Summer - a twelve day cruise of the Western Highlands, a ten day 'Round the North of Scotland' tour and a twelve day tour 'Round Great Britain' [31].

Valerie Burton's study of Liverpool's coastal trade in the mid nineteenth century provides a useful snapshot by taking statistics from the Liverpool Customs Bills of Entry for three separate months in 1853. It is difficult to compare like with like, however, as there is different information for arrivals and departures [32]). By tonnage of vessels, the Scottish traffic accounted for a little over 40 per cent of all the coastal trade with English, Scottish and Welsh ports. (Trade with Ireland - where there was no alternative to seaborne traffic - accounted for by far the greatest percentage of coastal traffic).

The function of Liverpool as an entrepot becomes very clear, as the forwarding of commodities imported into Liverpool from overseas to all coastal destinations overwhelmingly accounts for Liverpool's exports at the time. Examples were guano from South America which was forwarded to farming areas in southern Scotland [33]. Nevertheless, salt from Cheshire was a major export from Liverpool, almost half of it going to Scotland. Much of it went to the many small fishing ports in the north of

Scotland but the salt works at Cockenzie and St. Monans which were established to extract salt from seawater were increasingly using Cheshire salt [34].

Commodities shipped from Scotland included timber and timber products (pit props, staves, railway sleepers and larchwood planks) from Dumfries and Galloway. Some was used locally in the shipbuilding and furniture industries of Merseyside and in nearby coalmines, some was transhipped for onward journeys by sea or by rail. Gunpowder was shipped from Glasgow and Leith for the mines and slate quarries of South Lancashire and North Wales [35]. It seems that Galloway sheep were also brought to Liverpool as there is a reference to the Lancaster and Carlisle Railway (later the London and North Western Railway) attempting to undercut the rates offered by steamers [36]. In 1867, the L.N.W.R.'s rates for the carriage of livestock between southern Scotland and Liverpool were the second lowest in the country, the lowest being on the east coast (Great Northern, North Eastern and North British Railways) route from Aberdeen to London, which faced similar competition from steamships [37].

Although Glasgow was a major international port itself, it is an indication of Liverpool's importance as an entrepot that both pig iron and cast iron were brought from the Clyde ports to be re-exported to overseas markets [38].

Somewhat ironically, a significant amount of coastal trade between Liverpool and Scotland was through another English port, namely Silloth on the Solway. It has been seen that there was very little coastal traffic to the ports in eastern Scotland; this area was largely served by the North British Railway which was keen to develop an outlet for trade to Liverpool, Ireland and the Isle of Man. The N.B.R. had already reached Carlisle and, on 1 August 1862, it leased the line from Carlisle to Silloth, from where a fast screw steamer already operated a twice weekly service to Liverpool. The N.B.R. formed a subsidiary, the North British Steam Packet Company, which acquired the vessel and increased the weekly sailings to three. In 1866, another vessel was acquired and the service operated daily [39].

Silloth's hinterland was not limited to eastern Scotland. Railways also brought goods from the Eden valley, the Tyne valley and Carlisle itself but much traffic reached Silloth via the N.B.R.'s 'Waverley' route from Edinburgh. Paul Rees suggests that the railway's special rates for the carriage of some types of freight between certain towns and Liverpool indicate the major patterns of traffic. They include bacon from Dundee; ale, grate blocks, bags and bagging, whisky, meal, sugar and paper from Edinburgh; feedstuffs from Hawick; hemp and tow from Kirkcaldy; and sugar and cake from Perth. The company was also able to share in the movement of sheep from Dumfries-shire being brought across the Solway by boat for trans-shipment at Silloth[40]. Traffic declined towards the end of the century, sailings to Liverpool being reduced to three per week in 1891 and ending altogether in 1917[41].

The social significance of this trade for Merseyside probably lies in the fact that turnround time for ships was much longer at that time and there is anecdotal evidence that visiting Scots seamen made contacts in Liverpool and were particularly welcomed by the Scots community. Stories were told of Malcolm Mackinnon, headmaster of the Wesleyan School in Liverpool in the early years of the twentieth century. He and his wife were natives of the Isle of Skye and their first language was Gaelic. It was said that all seafarers from the Western Isles knew that they would always be sure of a welcome at the Mackinnon home in Upper Parliament Street, whenever they docked in Liverpool, so that there were frequent informal ceilidhs there[42].

Commerce and Manufacturing

In the later nineteenth century, manufacturing industries based on the processing of imported materials, especially sugar, tobacco and grain, developed on a large scale around the docks of Liverpool and Birkenhead, and Scots took full advantage of the opportunities presented. A good example is the firm of Macleod and Reid, who began as leaf tobacco merchants and importers in Glasgow in 1877. They opened a Liverpool office at 11 Redcross Street in 1887 and transferred the whole company to Liverpool in 1901; they became a limited company, although there were still both a Macleod and a Reid on the board, at least until 1927[43].

Whilst Cope Brothers, who also processed tobacco, were not Scots, at least one of their employees deserves mention, if only for his contribution to commercial art. John Fraser was born in Wick but began to work for Cope Brothers at a young age. From 1870 to 1900, he was secretary of the printing and publishing department and, during this period, his department produced a series of posters which were works of art in themselves; a large collection of them has survived in a special collection at Liverpool University. They are too numerous to be described in detail here but a few examples include a series of cartoons on the theme of golf ('Keep your eye on the ball......keep your eye on Cope's), 'Diva Nicotina' (with apologies to the painter of 'The Pursuit of Pleasure'), and one showing a crowd looking suspiciously like the Canterbury Pilgrims, on a pilgrimage to the shrine of St. Nicotinus. Other more serious themes included interior views of the Cope factory in Lord Nelson Street. Cope's also produced cigarette cards, usually with a literary theme and including 'Dickens Gallery', 'Shakespeare Gallery' and 'Characters from Scott'.

From March 1870 to January 1881, John Fraser edited Cope's house magazine, intended for both manufacturers and smokers, entitled *Tobacco Plant*. This included a number of literary articles, including one from John Ruskin (which resulted in a legal action for breach of copyright) and a series of illustrated articles on 'Pipes and Meerschaum'. Subscribers to *Tobacco Plant* received a calendar of poster size.

Fraser's obituary in *Cigar and Tobacco World* on 1 March 1902 described him as a Socialist and Fabian and member of the Church of Humanity (See Note One at end of chapter), but stated that 'his extreme opinions were always held with moderation' - something of a paradox. Could anyone but a Scot have elevated tobacco smoking to an art form? [44]

One of Liverpool's great characters was Robert Buchanan, son of James Buchanan, who had a corn mill at Tradeston, in Glasgow. After a short but interesting career as a cowboy in Texas, where it is said that he once helped a horse thief to escape, he returned to Scotland and eventually came to Liverpool as owner of Molyneaux' Mill (later known as Kirkdale Roller Mills), which he ran with his brother, William. They soon realised that a vacant site on the Wallasey side of Birkenhead Pool (the East Float) offered advantages over the Kirkdale site. At that time, urban expansion in Wirral was increasing demand for flour whilst, at the same time, decreasing supply by encroaching on agricultural land. Grain warehouses were established on Wallasey Pool, initially to supply imported grain to the windmills which were then found all over the Wirral, but the warehouses soon attracted flour mills, which were built close to them. Buchanan's new mill was burnt down in 1895, very soon after it was built, but was soon replaced, with the most modern equipment installed. By 1901, the mill's capacity was 10 tons per hour.

Robert Buchanan was elected Vice President of the Corn Trade Association in 1907 but resigned after a year, owing to pressure of work. He was an active member of the Volunteers, had been a member of the Glasgow Highlanders, and joined the Liverpool Scottish, acting as quartermaster during training at Blackpool during the First World War. He retired to Bosbury, Herefordshire and eventually left several hundred acres of his estate to the nation. He died on 18th February 1920 at Pau, France[45].

In the other important Merseyside industry of sugar refining, two Scots families, the Macfies and the Fairries, were particularly prominent. There is a record of a sugar bakery in Liverpool as early as 1673, so this was already a well established industry in the town. J. Leslie Fairrie opened a refinery in Greenock in 1797 and his sons also established refineries, the older son in London, the second son, Robert, in Liverpool. The Liverpool refinery was a seven storey building, established in 1847, at 231 Vauxhall Road. The Greenock refinery closed in 1858 and the London refinery by 1882, when all operations of Fairrie and Company Ltd, as the firm was known from 1866, were based at Liverpool[46].

Macfie and Sons was a family firm of sugar refiners which also originated in Greenock in 1788 and spread to Leith. In 1838, the firm moved into Liverpool, purchasing Hutchinson's refinery in Temple Street, followed by Wainwright and Company's refinery in Batchelor Street in 1841 and William Street refinery in 1846. Like Fairrie's, they closed their Scottish plants shortly afterwards, in 1852. By 1864, Macfie's was producing 500 tons of soft sugar weekly and had become the largest producer in Britain.

This pre-eminence was not, however, to last. In fact, both Fairrie's and Macfie's were soon to be overtaken by and later absorbed by Tate and Lyle. By 1900, there were only 16 sugar refining companies in Britain, with Henry Tate of Liverpool and Lyle (still a separate firm on Clydeside) accounting for 62.5 per cent of total output between them. The comparative success of Tate's was due to their adaptability to changed circumstances. In the latter part of the nineteenth century, there was a rise in the price of imported cane sugar, to which Macfie's responded by using beet sugar in plant unsuited to it and with staff inexperienced in its handling; they also opened new refineries, such as Rawcliffe, near Goole, with better access to the beet growing areas.

Tate, on the other hand, invested in new technology such as the Boivin Loise process, which improved the quality and purity of sugar, and in the Langen process for making cube sugar - a new product. Macfie's did not introduce the Langen process until about twenty years later, by which time it had already been superseded by another process at Tate's[47]. Tate and Lyle acquired Fairrie's in 1929 and Macfie's in 1938[48].

Scots were prominent in many other aspects of Liverpool's trade. Fire insurance was obviously important to the citizens and tradesmen of a town like Liverpool and, in June 1802, the famous Dr. James Currie (discussed in Chapter Four), together with his friends, William Rathbone and George Booth, another Unitarian shipowner, took the lead in establishing the Liverpool St. George's Fire Office in premises on the corner of Water Street and Exchange Alley. Another Liverpool Scot amongst the 26 proprietors was William Ewart, a friend of Sir John Gladstone. Although there were several agents for insurance companies in Liverpool, the only previous Liverpool company had been the Liverpool Fire Office, established in 1776 but which went out of business before the turn of the century. Unfortunately, the St. George's Office had even less success, as there was a major fire in Goree Piazzas in September 1802, only three months after its formation. 17 warehouses were destroyed and the cost to the St. George's Office was £323,000 - a financial blow from which it never really recovered. It failed in 1806[49].

James Aikin was a Liverpool Scots merchant and shipbroker, who played a major part in Liverpool's development as a major centre of marine insurance. He floated the Union Marine Insurance Company in January 1863 and was appointed its first chairman, but retired two years later[50]. He too played an active part in the general life of the town. He was a magistrate and a Liberal candidate at Liverpool's first municipal election in 1835. He took a particular interest in the School for the Blind and the Liverpool Shipwreck and Humane Society[51]. He was also (with William Roscoe) a joint founder of the Royal Institution and Liverpool Philomathic Society[52].

One of Liverpool's best known firms was Fawcett Preston, who made marine engines, including a 22 hp engine for the *Etna*, the first steam ferry on the Mersey. This company owed its beginnings to George Perry, who was born in Scotland in 1719 and, after considering a career in the church, went to work for Abraham Darby's Coalbrookdale Ironworks. In 1758, he was sent to manage their branch at 17 York Street, Liverpool; this was virtually a warehouse for their iron kettles and pots, whose weight resulted in high transport costs. It therefore made economic sense for them to be manufactured near to their market and the Phoenix Foundry was added on the Liverpool site. When Abraham Darby faced some financial difficulty, the Liverpool operation was acquired by George Rathbone and later by his nephew, William Fawcett. Although George Perry did not see the firm reach pre-eminence in marine engineering, it owed its origins to him [53].

Commercial Benefactors

Some indication of the extent of Scots' participation in the commerce of Liverpool came in 1882, when University College, Liverpool was founded. One of its most enthusiastic benefactors was William Rathbone, the grandson of James Currie's friend. He describes his efforts to raise funds to establish chairs in the new college, stating:

> I then went to Mr. Balfour and Mr. Samuel Smith, as Scotchmen, and pointed out that, as the Scotch had been fifty years ahead of us in education, and with the good education they had, many of them came to Liverpool and realised good fortunes - it would be a graceful thing if the Scotch merchants of Liverpool would found a Professorship of Political Economy and Moral Philosophy, two subjects often joined in Scotch Universities. To this they agreed and raised the necessary funds for it [54].

The first Calendar of University College shows that 41 Scots merchants did subscribe a total of £10,000 to found the Chair of Philosophy, Logic and Political Economy, as it was known (See Note Two at end of chapter). They seem to have been particularly representative of the trade of the port, especially the cotton and woollen trades. R. W. Ronald, for example, contributed £100 personally, whilst his firm of woolbrokers gave another £50. One of the most generous benefactors was Samuel Smith, who gave £1,000 himself, whilst his firm of cotton brokers, Smith, Edwards and Co. contributed a further £500 [55].

Samuel Smith, the Cotton King of Liverpool, was one of the town's greatest philanthropists. He must have been one of the very few people to have had a totally uncritical article about himself in Liverpool's satirical periodical, *The Porcupine*, which was scathing of most people. Born in Borgue, Kirkcudbrightshire, in 1835, he went to Edinburgh University, intending to become a 'minister of the Lord' but decided to enter the world of business instead. He came to Liverpool in 1858 and became a member of the Canning Street Kirk congregation. After spending some time in the USA, familiarising himself with cotton, he returned to Liverpool to establish the firm of Smith, Edwards and Co., cotton brokers. He later went to India on behalf of the Cotton Brokers Association to study cotton there. This was of particular value to Liverpool, as first the cotton famine caused by the American Civil War and, second, the opening of the Suez Canal both led to a considerable rise in imports of cotton from India. He then became a partner in Messrs Finlay and Co., cotton merchants.

Smith was a man of literary talents and his works included *Occasional Essays* and *The Credibility of the Christian Religion*. His Christianity was essentially one of "deeds not words". Much of his philanthropy was anonymous but he is believed to have contributed between £8,000 and £10,000 a year (about a third of his income) to various causes, including probably £20,000 to the YMCA gymnasium. When accused of supporting Mrs. Birt's Sheltering Homes, which allegedly subverted Roman Catholic children, he replied, "No, I subscribe to feed the starving and destitute" and offered to donate equal sums to a similar Catholic charity, an offer taken up by Fr. Nugent who was the undisputed pioneer of Catholic social work in Liverpool[56].

He was particularly keen to bring culture to the working classes and would entertain young women shopworkers to musical evenings after dinner at the best restaurants in town. He hired a theatre, known as the Colosseum, in Paradise Street to put on entertainments 'free of objectionable features' on weekdays, and evangelistic services on Sundays, though the unobjectionable entertainments do not seem to have been very popular. Children attending Sunday School at the Colosseum each received a loaf[57].

Samuel Smith also built the Gordon Smith Institute for Seamen in Paradise Street, with a library, reading room and clubrooms for the Liverpool Seaman's Friends Society (a charity established in 1820 'to promote......the happiness of seamen and their families') and the Gordon Hall for the Y.W.C.A in Blackburne Place - both named in memory of his son[58]. During his visit to New York, he had witnessed the work amongst child victims of abuse, and in 1883, he helped T. F. Agnew to found the Liverpool Society for the Prevention of Cruelty to Children, the forerunner of the national society.

In 1878, he was elected to the City Council and in December 1882, he defeated A. B. Forwood to become Liberal M.P. for Liverpool, which had always been considered a Tory stronghold. It seems that his generosity to Catholic charities and earlier denials of accusations of proselytising had been accepted, as priests advised their congregations to vote for him. As a result of boundary changes, he lost the seat in 1885, but was later elected as member for Flintshire, holding the seat until his death in 1906 [59]. *The Porcupine* commented that, if he had given as much to political causes as he had to charity, Liverpool would long ago have been a Liberal town.

The list of benefactors of the University College chair included Alexander Balfour, who was also involved with many charitable causes. He was very concerned about the effects of excessive drinking in Liverpool and was prominent in the temperance movement. Once, when returning from a business trip to South America, in 1867, he learned that two of the crew had died on the voyage and concern for their families led him to found the Seaman's Orphanage in Newsham Park, a very fine Gothic building designed by Waterhouse. Like Smith, he was a very active supporter of Louisa Birt's Sheltering Homes and it was he who invited her sister to come to Liverpool to speak at a meeting to set it up [60]. In 1881, he was anxious about Louisa Birt's health and paid for her and her sister to visit the Mediterranean. He also owned a cottage on the Mount Alyn estate, Rossett, which was known as 'the minister's cottage', as ministers and their wives were always welcome to take a break there [61].

Another name on the list of University College's Scots benefactors also took an interest in the Sheltering Homes, Mr. Henry Cox being the first to contribute to the Girls' Sheltering Home [62]. John Rankin was Chairman of several Liverpool companies, including the Royal Insurance Company, Pacific Steam Navigation and the Bank of Liverpool. His generosity to the University did not end with his contribution to the Chair of Philosophy, Logic and Political Economy and spanned a very wide range of academic disciplines. He was one of a number of businessmen who funded the Institute of Archaeology and, in 1905, personally funded a special lectureship in Methods and Practice of Archaeology, providing further funds the following year to establish a chair. In 1908, he established the Chair of Modern History and supplemented the money from a bequest from the late John L. Bowes to establish the Chair in Russian History, Language and Literature, the first in the country. In 1917, he partly endowed the Chair of Geography (fully endowing it three years later) and in 1919, together with E. K. Muspratt, made a gift which allowed a second Chair of English Literature to be set up. Also in 1919, he and George Rathbone made it possible for a part-time lectureship in Music to become full time and in the same year contributed to a Special Lectureship in Poetry. The duties of these two lectureships included public lectures. Finally, in 1920, he established a Chair in the Thermodynamics of Heat Engines in the Faculty of Engineering, in memory of his son Robert. Not surprisingly, one of the University's first halls of residence was named Rankin Hall, in Ullet Road, and when it closed, was replaced by a new hall of the same name on the Carnatic campus site [63]. His total contributions to various causes, not only the University, were estimated at about a million pounds [64].

Finally, another Scots businessman and benefactor of Liverpool was James Smith. Born in Paisley in 1831, he moved with his family first to Kingstown (now Dun Laoghaire) in 1836 and then to Bootle in 1851. He set up a successful business as a wine merchant. Although largely self-educated, he had broad interests in music, literature, philosophy, Egyptology and especially art. He was a personal friend of Rodin and the painter G. F. Watts. He acquired several of their works which he bequeathed to the Walker Art Gallery, together with several of David Williamson's water colours.

James Smith left £30,000 each to the Liverpool Institute to establish eight entrance scholarships (five for boys and three for girls), and to Liverpool University for scholarships to pupils from the Institute schools. They were known as the Margaret Bryce Smith scholarships, in memory of his mother [65].

St.Helens

East of Liverpool lies St. Helens, famous for a variety of industries, notably coalmining, alkalis and soap, glass, and engineering - and Scots played a prominent part in the development of all of them. John Mackay opened the Thatto Heath mines in 1771 and two years later saw a market for British-made plate glass, which had previously been imported almost entirely from St. Gobain in France. In 1773, the British Cast Plate Glass Company (later known as John Mackay and Co.) was established at Ravenhead, naturally using coal from Mackay's mines. In the 1880s, Mackay made an attempt to manufacture stained and enamelled glass in Liverpool [66].

Local coal and access to Cheshire salt by waterway attracted the alkali and soap industry to the banks of the Sankey Canal - the first works being established in 1828, by Muspratt and Gamble. Though an Ulsterman, from County Fermanagh by birth, Josias Christopher Gamble had read theology at Glasgow. He had intended to enter the Presbyterian ministry but became interested in chemistry and made a career in industry instead. Before long, the alkali industry was facing litigation because of the pollution which was causing considerable environmental damage. This could be minimised by condensing hydrochloric acid gas in 'Gossage towers'.

To erect these towers at Gamble and Crosfields (as the company was now known) and other alkali works in the town, Gossages sent a Scot, James Shanks. He had studied medicine at Glasgow but, like Gamble, had acquired an interest in chemistry and entered industry. In 1840, Gamble appointed him as manager and, by 1868, he had quadrupled the rateable value of the company [67].

Another prominent Scot was James McBryde of Stranraer who came to St. Helens to work as a chemist for Gamble in 1847, at the age of 21. In the 1860s, he went into partnership with Llewellyn William to build a new alkali works at Pocket Nook, buying his partner's share in 1873, after which the company was known as James McBryde and Co. Ltd. [68].

The Bridgewater Smelting Company was established, about 1853, by Thomas Watson, who formerly worked in the silk trade in Paisley, (in partnership with John Wilson and John Knowles Leathers), to manufacture copper and sulphuric acid from copper pyrites. There was a close link between copper and alkali trades and an alkali works was also built nearby. Unfortunately, the company did not survive the depression of the 1870s and was bankrupt by 1878; its plant was auctioned in 1884 [69].

Scotland also provided pioneers for St. Helens's metallurgical and engineering industries. George Scott's Caledonian Foundry in Crosfield Street was an iron and brass foundry, which made horizontal and vertical steam engines and pumps for the alkali works [70]. The Bridgewater Forge (later the St. Helens Ironworks) in Watson Street was originally owned by Pilkington's but Hadden William Todd of Aberdeen became a partner in 1859. When Richard Pilkington retired, Charles Todd joined the firm which was then known as Todd Brothers [71]. In 1871, Duncan McKechnie of Campbeltown had a difference of opinion with his partner in Runcorn and set up a copper smelting works in St. Helens [72].

Conclusion

As noted earlier, Scottish entrepreneurship was extremely important in the development of business concerns elsewhere and Scottish investment was particularly important in the areas of finance, shipping and industry. Liverpool, with its port and its export links with the Americas clearly represented an important opportunity for Scots investors and it should be no surprise that Scots played such an important role in the development of shipping and shipbuilding on

Merseyside. Influence was not, of course, confined solely to the port and other local industries benefited from a Scots input.

Interestingly, it is not immediately clear that Scotland itself benefited from this investment. There is evidence that investment in the former colonies provided a stimulus to trade and to manufacturing at home [73] but investment in England may not have had the same effect. It is notable that the greatest impact by Scots on Merseyside commercial development was in the late eighteenth and nineteenth centuries, as the numbers of Scots businessmen coming to the area seems to have declined after 1918. Indeed, Campbell makes the point that emigration to non-European destinations fell dramatically after the First World War with Scots tending instead to take 'Dr. Johnson's road to England' [74], the implication being that this created a problem for Scotland. When Scots at home needed markets pioneered by Scots abroad, in the 1930s, they became less available.

Scots businessmen do not seem to have been particularly sentimental and, as Campbell points out, 'The emigrant Scot may have succeeded because his affection for his native land was never allowed to interfere with his own commercial judgement'[75].
In this respect, the Scots were quite different from for example the Irish, whose industrial role was much more one of worker rather than investor. Ultimately, perhaps, the Scots have made more of a lasting mark on the Merseyside industrial scene.

References

1. C.Harvie (1994), Scotland and Nationalism. Scottish Society and Politics 1707-1994 (Second Edition), Routledge, London, p.69.
2. R.H.Campbell (1985), 'Scotland' in R.A.Cage (ed.), The Scots Abroad. Labour, Capital, Enterprise 1750-1914, Croom Helm, London, p.19.
3. Quoted in Harvie (1994), Op. cit., p.57.
4. I.Donnachie (1992), 'The Making of "Scots on the Make": Scottish Settlement and Enterprise in Australia, 1830-1900' in T.M.Devine (ed.), Scottish Emigration and Scottish Society, John Donald, Edinburgh, p.147.
5. R.H.Campbell (1985), Op. cit., pp.20-21.
6. George Chandler (1972), An Illustrated History of Liverpool, p.97.
7. David Wainwright (1960), Liverpool Gentlemen, p.18.
8. Robert Griffiths (1923), The History of the Royal and Ancient Park of Toxteth, Liverpool, p.99.

9. David Wainwright, Op. cit., pp.22, 29, 31, 49.

10. (i) F.E.Hyde (1971), Liverpool and the Mersey, p.52.
    (ii) A Second Merseyside Maritime History, Liverpool Nautical History Society, (1991), p.17.

11. (i) F.E.Hyde, Op. cit., pp.84-87.
    (ii) Sir David J. Owen (1948), Ports of the United Kingdom, p.71.

12. Paul Rees (1984), Guide to Merseyside's Past, p.37.

13. Nikolaus Pevsner and Edward Hubbard (1971), Buildings of England: Cheshire, p.76.

14. F.E.Hyde, Op. cit., p.61.

15. (i) P.N.Davies (1978), Sir Alfred Jones, pp.21-30, 38 and 49.
    (ii) Shipping - A Survey of Historical Records (1971), p.48.
    (iii) F.E.Hyde, Op. cit., p.61.

16. Mersey Docks and Harbour Board (1935-6), The Port of Liverpool, Liverpool: Littlebury Bros., pp.146-7

17. (i) St. Andrew's Kirk, Rodney Street, Liverpool, unpublished paper.
    (ii) Second Maritime History pp.33-34.

18. (i) Ibid, p.35.
    (ii) Shipping: Hist. Records, p.44.

19. The Porcupine, 21 May 1864.

20. Shipping: Hist. Records, p.44.

21. Second Maritime History, p.36.

22. David Wainwright, Op. cit., p.101.

23. Ibid., p.37.

24. Clement Jones (1938), Pioneer Shipowners, Vol II, p.97.

25. G. Chandler (1960), Liverpool Shipping, London: Phoenix House, p.47

26. R.B. Mooney (1969), 'A Business Journey from Orkney to Liverpool in 1789', Transactions of the Historic Society of Lancashire and Cheshire, vol. 121

27. Gore's Liverpool Directories 1818 and 1851

28. Chandler, Op. cit., pp. 53-55

29. Ibid, p.56

30. (i) R.R. Cunningham (1974), Portpatrick through the Ages, Wigtown Free Press, p.16
    (ii) R.R. Cunningham (1977), Portpatrick and its Lifeboat 1877-1977, Wigtown Free Press, p.1

31. Bradshaw's Railway Guide 1910, pp.949 and 951. (Reprinted Newton Abbot: David and Charles, 1968)

32. V. Burton (1989), 'Liverpool's mid-Nineteenth Century Coasting Trade' in

Liverpool Shipping, Trade and Industry, National Museums and Galleries on Merseyside, pp.52-61.

33. Ibid, p.46.

34. Ibid, pp 45, 48 and 50.

35. Ibid, p.40

36. Ibid, p.43

37. G. Channon (1969), 'The Aberdeenshire Beef Trade with London', Transport History, vol. II, p.6

38. Burton, Op. cit., p.36.

39. P. Rees (1994), 'North British Railway Steamer Services between Silloth and Liverpool' in Docks, Railways and the Movement of Goods, Merseyside Maritime Museum, pp.19-20.

40. Ibid, pp.28-29

41. Ibid, pp.24-26.

42. Personal reminiscences, Mrs. M. I. Munro and others

43. 'Foundations of Liverpool's Greatness - Docks and Shipping', Supplement to Liverpool Daily Post, 19th July 1927.

44. Material in the James Fraser Collection, Liverpool University.

45. G.J.S. Broomhall and J.H. Hubback (1930), 'Memories of Individuals and Firms' in Corn Trade Memories, pp. 75-78.

46. J.A.Watson (1973), A Hundred Years of Sugar Refining, p.48.

47. A. Murray (1983), 'A Staple Consumer Industry in Liverpool - Sugar Refining in the Nineteenth Century' in B.L.Anderson and P.J.M.Stoney (eds), Commerce, Industry and Transport. Studies in Economic Change on Merseyside, pp.62-65.

48. J.A.Watson, Op. cit., p.4.

49. P.C.Brown (1926), 'Fire Insurance in Liverpool', Transactions of the Historic Society of Lancashire and Cheshire, vol.78, pp.3-20.

50. Union Marine Insurance Company, 1863-1913, (1913).

51. Liberal Review, 13th July 1878.

52. Liverpolitana, (1971), p.73.

53. (i) Ibid., pp.102-103.
(ii) Sea Breezes, vol. 26 (September 1958).

54. Thomas Kelly (1981), For the Advancement of Learning. The University of Liverpool, 1881-1981, pp.47-49, quoting William Rathbone's 'Sketch of Family History'.

55. (i) Calendar, University College,Liverpool, 1882.
(ii) Gore's Directory of Liverpool, 1881.

56. (i) The Porcupine, 2nd December 1882.

(ii) 'Louisa Birt: Children's Home Finder' in <u>Liverpool Citizen</u>, 14 January 1883, p.151.
57. <u>Ibid.</u>, p.155.
58. Gore's <u>Directory of Liverpool</u>.
59. (i) Liverpolitana, p.146
    (ii) A. F. Richardson (1990), <u>Well, I Never Noticed That</u>, Liverpool: West Derby Publishing, part 1, pp.60-61.
60. (i) <u>Buildings of Liverpool</u>, (1978), Liverpool Heritage Bureau, p.144.
    (ii) 'Louisa Birt', <u>Op. cit.</u>, pp.109-111.
61. <u>Ibid.</u>, pp.149-150.
62. <u>Ibid.</u>, p.154.
63. Thomas Kelly, <u>Op. cit.</u>, various references.
64 <u>Liverpolitana</u> (1971), p.7.
65. H. J. Tiffin (1935), <u>History of the Liverpool Institute Schools</u>, Liverpool Institute Old Boys Association, p.177.
66. (i) T.C.Barker and J.R.Harris (1954), <u>St. Helens: A Merseyside Town in the Industrial Revolution. St. Helens, 1750-1900</u>, Liverpool U.P., pp.112-113.
    (ii) Nikolaus Pevsner (1969), <u>The Buildings of England: South Lancashire</u>, p.383.
67. Barker and Harris, <u>Op. cit.</u>, pp.227-228 and 236-237.
68. <u>Ibid.</u>, p.345.
69. <u>Ibid.</u>, p.346.
70. (i) <u>Ibid.</u>, p.365.
    (ii) Advertisement in <u>St. Helens Standard</u>, 28th April 1866.
71. Barker and Harris, <u>Op. cit.</u>, p.365.
72. <u>Ibid.</u>, p.436.
73. R.H.Campbell (1985), <u>Op. cit.</u>
74. <u>Ibid.</u>, p.24
75. <u>Ibid.</u>, p.25

Note One

The Church of Humanity was founded by Auguste Comte, who rejected everything which could not be proved by scientific phenomena, but recognised that Christianity had played an important historical role and fulfilled an emotional need. He set up a church, in which the deity was identified with humanity and had a system of worship analogous to the Catholic calendar and ritual. The Liverpool church in Upper Parliament Street is still standing but is now owned by the Christian Scientists.

Note Two

SCOTS MERCHANTS CONTRIBUTING TO THE FOUNDATION OF THE
CHAIR OF PHILOSOPHY, LOGIC AND POLITICAL ECONOMY AT
UNIVERSITY COLLEGE, LIVERPOOL, 1882. .

	£
Messrs Balfour, Williamson and Co., merchants.	2,000
D. Jardine, esq., timber merchant	1,000
J. Rew, cotton broker	1,000
Samuel Smith, esq., cotton broker	1,000
James Cox, esq.	500
David Duncan, esq., merchant	500
H. H. Nicholson, esq., cotton broker	500
Messrs Smith, Edwards and Co., cotton brokers	500
Samuel Stitt, esq., stockbroker?	500
James Smith, esq.	250
Hyslop Maxwell, esq.	200
Messrs Smith, Wood and Co., East India merchants	150
Messrs M'Diarmid and Greenshields, shipowners, merchants and shipbrokers	150
Henry Cox, esq., oil refiner (Phoenix Mill)?	150
Robert Rankin, esq., merchant	100
Messrs Moffat Bros., cotton and general brokers	100
John Roxburgh, esq., cotton broker	100
George R. Cox, esq.	100
L. H. McIntyre, esq.	100
Messrs W. H. Ross and Co., merchants	100
R. A. Macfie, esq., sugar refiner	100
George Cockbain, esq., artist	100
Alex. Robertson, esq., engineer?	100
Messrs A. Hannay and Co., corn merchants	100
J. Watson Bell, esq., agent for tea merchant?	100
R. W. Ronald, esq., woolbroker	100
Messrs Ronald, Sons and Co., woolbrokers	50
Robert Allan, esq.	50
William Nichol, esq., cotton broker	50

W. G. Henderson, esq.	50
Messrs Urquhart and Adamson, cabinet makers,	
upholsterers, glass manufacturers and exporters	25
Andrew Boyd, esq. (gentleman)	25
John Marquis, esq., broker?	25
H. J. Wallace, esq., underwriter?	25
A. Gillies, esq., engineer?	25
William McGregor, esq.	25
Thomas Mills, esq.	20
Messrs Richardson, Dunlop and Co., tailors and drapers	20
Thomas Irvine, esq., stock and share broker?	20
Henry Coubrough, esq., merchant	20
Andrew Callender, esq., provision merchant?	20

These names and subscriptions are listed in the first University College Calendar of 1882. An attempt was made to check the subscribers' occupations in Gores' Directories for the period. This was only partially successful, since there was frequently found to be more than one person of the same name, and general descriptions such as "merchant" and "broker" are not sufficiently helpful. It does, however, give some indication that Scots were particularly prominent in port-related trades associated with imports and commerce.

Statue of Alexander Balfour, Scots merchant and philanthropist

Love Lane refinery: 1875

The barque *Martina Johanna* (1,360 nett tons) unloading a cargo of Java sugar

The Seamen's orphanage in Newsham Park is an example of Alexander Balfour's generosity

STEAM COMMUNICATION
BETWEEN
LIVERPOOL AND GLASGOW.

REDUCTION OF FARES:
Cabin, 10s.; Steward's Fee, 2s.; Steerage, 5s.

THE GLASGOW AND LIVERPOOL STEAM SHIPPING COMPANY'S NEW STEAM SHIPS,
ORION .... Capt. HENDERSON,
COMMODORE.. ..... (Chartered)........ Capt. ——.
THE GLASGOW AND LIVERPOOL ROYAL STEAM PACKET COMPANY'S STEAMER,
PRINCESS ROYAL .... Capt. CRAWFORD.
THE CITY OF GLASGOW STEAM PACKET COMPANY'S STEAMER,
ADMIRAL.......... Capt. HARDIE.

Or other Steam Ships, are intended to Sail between Glasgow and Liverpool, with Goods and Passengers, as under :

From Liverpool. (Sailing from Clarence Dock.) MARCH, 1850.	*From Glasgow.* Passengers leaving Glasgow by the Railway Trains at the hours noted below, will be in time to join the Vessel at Greenock. MARCH, 1850.		By Rail.
ORION .... Saturday 2nd.. 12 noon	ADMIRAL........... Saturday 2nd..	12 noon	3 p.m.
ADMIRAL........ Tuesday 5th.. 3 p.m.	ORION .... Tuesday 5th..	3 p.m.	6 ,,
ORION .... Thursday 7th.. 4 ,,	ADMIRAL......... Thursday 7th..	5 ,,	7 —
ADMIRAL........ Saturday 9th.. 8 ,,	ORION .... Saturday 9th..	7 ,,	—
ORION .... Tuesday 12th.. 8½ ,,	PRINCESS ROYAL. Tuesday 12th..	10 a.m.	12 noon
PRINCESS ROYAL. Thursday 14th.. 11 a.m.	ORION .... Thursday 14th..	11 ,,	2 p.m.
ORION .... Saturday 16th.. 11 ,,	PRINCESS ROYAL. Saturday 16th..	11 ,,	2 ,,
PRINCESS ROYAL. Tuesday 19th.. 2 p.m.	ORION .... Tuesday 19th..	1 p.m.	4 ,,
ORION .... Thursday 21st.. 2½ ,,	PRINCESS ROYAL.. Thursday 21st..	3 ,,	6 ,,
PRINCESS ROYAL. Saturday 23rd.. 5 ,,	ORION .... Saturday 23rd..	5 ,,	7 ,,
COMMODORE .... Tuesday 26th.. 9 ,,	PRINCESS ROYAL.. Tuesday 26th..	8 ,,	—
PRINCESS ROYAL. Thursday 28th.. 11 a.m.	COMMODORE....... Thursday 28th..	11 a.m.	2 p.m.
COMMODORE .... Saturday 30th.. 12 noon.	ADMIRAL .... Saturday 30th..	11 ,,	2 ,,

N.B.—Goods, Carriages, and Horses intended for Shipment require to be alongside the vessel at least one hour before the advertised time of sailing.

Rates of Freight by these Vessels include all Clyde Dues.
☞ Passengers are requested to take charge of their own luggage, as the ship is not responsible in any way for its safety.
All Goods carried by these Vessels, and which are to or from the Interior of England, &c., when consigned to the care of any of the Company's Agents in Liverpool, are forwarded free of all charge for Forwarding, Cartage, and Dues at Liverpool.

Agents for the "Orion" and "Commodore."	Agents for the "Admiral."	Agents for the "Princess Royal."
Aléx. M'Culloch, Excise-buildings, Greenock.	Lindsay & Co.; Excise-buildings, Greenock.	D. M'Larty & Co.; Excise-building, Greenock.
G. and J. Burns, 9, Buchanan-street, Glasgow.	Thomson and MacConnell, 14; Jamaica-street, Glasgow.	M. Langlands, 32, St. Enoch-sq., Glasgow.
Martin and Burns and Co., 7, Water-street, Liverpool.	David MacIvor and Co., 14, Water-street, Liverpool.	Robert Lamont, 83, Water-street, Liverpool.

J. B. Foord, 52, Old Broad-street. London.

Before the completion of the west coast railway line, coastal shipping was the main means of communication between Liverpool and Glasgow.
The "Orion" sank off Portpatrick with great loss of life a few months after this advertisment appeared.

GLASGOW AND LIVERPOOL
(Calling at GREENOCK, CUSTOM HOUSE QUAY).
Fast Steamships SPANIEL, POINTER, and WREN, or other Steamers.

Fares between Glasgow (Broomielaw) or Greenock and Liverpool:—Single Cabin, 11/6; Steerage, 6/-. Return, Cabin (valid for Two Months), 17/- ; (10 Days), 15/-.; Steerage (valid Ten Days), 8/6. Fares, between Glasgow (Central Station) and Liverpool, via Greenock, single, Cabin and 1st cl., 13/-; Steerage and 3rd cl., 6/9. Return, Cabin and 1st cl. (valid Two Months), 19/6; Cabin and 3rd cl. (valid Two Months), 18/6.

FROM GLASGOW			April.	FROM LIVERPOOL
Shed 14 (Broomielaw),	Central Station, by train to Greenock, where passengers can join the steamer at Custom House Quay.			**Prince's Dock (South-East Side)**
SPANIEL .... 4 0 p.m.	.... 8 30 p.m.	Friday 1st		POINTER .... *5 0 p.m.
WREN .. ..10 0 p.m.	....	Saturday 2nd		
GORILLA.............. 4 0 p.m.	.... 8 30 p.m.	Monday 4th		SPANIEL.................... 5 0 p.m.
		Tuesday .. 5th		WREN .... 7 0 p.m.
SPANIEL .... 4 0 p.m.	.... 8 30 p.m.	Wednesday 6th		GORILLA.................... 8 0 p.m.
WREN .... 4 0 p.m.	.... 8 30 p.m.	Thursday .. 7th		
GORILLA.............. 4 0 p.m.	.... 8 30 p.m.	Friday 8th		SPANIEL.................... 9 30 p.m.
		Saturday 9th		WREN ....10 0 p.m.
SPANIEL .... 4 0 p.m.	.... 7 10 p.m.	Monday 11th		GORILLA ....11 0 p.m.
WREN .... 4 0 p.m.	.... 8 30 p.m.	Tuesday 12th		
GORILLA.............. 4 0 p.m.	.... 8 30 p.m.	Wednesday .. 13th		SPANIEL....................12 30 p.m.
		Thursday 14th		WREN .... 1 30 p.m.
SPANIEL .... 4 0 p.m.	.... 8 30 p.m.	Friday 15th		GORILLA.................... 2 0 p.m.
WREN .... 4 0 p.m.	.... 8 30 p.m.	Saturday 16th		
POINTER .... 4 0 p.m.	.... 8 30 p.m.	Monday 18th		SPANIEL.................... 6 0 p.m.
		Tuesday...... 19th		WREN .... 7 30 p.m.
SPANIEL .... 4 0 p.m.	.... 8 30 p.m.	Wednesday .. 20th		POINTER .... 8 0 p.m.
WREN .. .. 4 0 p.m.	.... 8 30 p.m.	Thursday 21st		
POINTER .... 4 0 p.m.	.... 8 30 p.m.	Friday 22nd		SPANIEL.................... 9 30 p.m.
		Saturday 23rd		WREN ....10 0 p.m.
SPANIEL .... 3 0 p.m.	.... 6 30 p.m.	Monday 25th		POINTER ....11 0 p.m.
WREN .... 4 0 p.m.	.... 7 10 p.m.	Tuesday 26th		
POINTER .... 4 0 p.m.	.... 7 10 p.m.	Wednesday ... 27th		SPANIEL....................11 0 p.m.
		Thursday..... 28th		WREN ....12 0 noon
SPANIEL .... 4 0 p.m.	.... 8 30 p.m.	Friday 29th		POINTER .... 1 0 p.m.
WREN .... 4 0 p.m.	.... 8 30 p.m.	Saturday 30th		

* From Landing Stage.

Return Tickets are only available by Messrs. BURNS' Steamers, and are not transferable.
THROUGH BOOKINGS by Steamer and Rail between **Glasgow, Greenock, and Manchester**, and other Stations, *via* Liverpool, in connection with Cheshire Lines Committee, L. & Y. Railway, and L. & N. W. Railway, for particulars of which apply at the Railway Offices in Liverpool and Manchester, or

G. & J. BURNS, Ltd., 2, Brymner Street, Greenock ; The Harbour, Ardrossan; Exchange Buildings, Liverpool; Londonderry; Larne; 49, Queen's Square, Belfast; and 30, Jamaica Street, Glasgow.   [J.R.

Coastal passenger ships were still operating well after the completion of the railway network for this 1910 advertisment shows

113

LANGLANDS'
Passenger and Cargo Steamers.

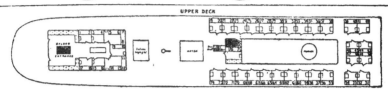

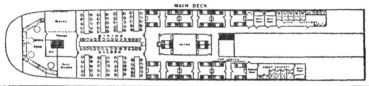

₁₂ DAY YACHTING CRUISES
TO
WEST HIGHLANDS (ᴺᴼ CARGO).

From LIVERPOOL, May 13th and 24th; June 4th, 17th, and 30th; July 14th and 27th; August 9th and 24th; and September 6th.

10 DAY TOURS Round North of Scotland.

From LIVERPOOL, WEEKLY (every Thursday), commencing in May.

12 DAY TOURS Round Great Britain (Without Change of Steamer.)

From LIVERPOOL, FORTNIGHTLY, commencing in June.

Fares from about 10s. per day including Breakfast, Lunch, Afternoon Tea, and Dinner, served on a most liberal basis.

Regular Service of Passenger and Cargo Steamers between Glasgow and Liverpool and Glasgow and Manchester.

PARTICULARS FREE FROM—

M. LANGLAND & SONS—(B. Dept.), Liverpool.
Telegrams: "LANGLANDS."   Telephone, 1487 Central.

M. Langlands' and Sons cruises to Scotland (a 1910 advertisment)

114

In the mid nineteenth century the Cunard Company (and much of Liverpool life)
was dominated by Charles MacIver (Walker Art Gallery)

Cunard's transatlantic operations began on Independence Day 1840 when the Britannia left Liverpool

CHAPTER SIX

The Liverpool Scottish

Introduction

As a nation, Scotland has a strong military tradition. Prior to the 1745 Rising, the Highland regiments were essentially clan-based and, for a time thereafter, military activity in the Highlands was banned as a fresh upsurge of Jacobitism was feared. But the demands of the British Empire, particularly in America where there were long periods of fighting against the French, and later the colonists themselves, led to a shortage of trained soldiers and recruitment in Scotland began to be encouraged. Soldiers from the Highland regiments subsequently distinguished themselves in action in North America, for example during Wolfe's Quebec campaign.

Colley, for example, speaks of Scotland as becoming the arsenal of the British Empire and quotes the Secretary of State for War, Lord Barrington, addressing Parliament in 1751:

> I am for having always in our army as many Scottish soldiers as possible; not that I think them more brave than those of any other country we can recruit from, but because they are generally more hardy and less mutinous: and of all Scottish soldiers I should choose to have and keep in our army as many Highlanders as possible [1].

Scottish soldiers were generally well educated and created a military literature. There were stories of bravery and glamour and each war produced its heroes, including Moore at Corunna, Ensign Ewart at Waterloo and the 'Thin Red Line' at Balaclava [2]. The Scottish infantry, 'the ladies from hell', personified Scotland at its most aggressive. In fact, the proportion of Scots in the Victorian army was never higher than 1:7 and was often lower than this, but the reputation was of Scottish bravery and intelligence compensating for the incompetence or cowardice of English officers [3].

Most Scottish regiments were, naturally enough, raised in Scotland but the military tradition was taken elsewhere by expatriate Scots and, within England, there were Scottish regiments established in London, Liverpool and Newcastle. This chapter focuses on the Liverpool Scottish.

The Raising of the Company

In the years following the Crimean War, there was considerable interest in the

Volunteers, not least amongst expatriate Scots in England. The London Scottish (15th Middlesex Rifle Volunteer Corps) was raised in 1859 and the same year, similar efforts were made in Liverpool. Liverpool Scots were, of course, already well represented in existing volunteer corps of rifles, engineers and artillery before a proposal to raise a company, to be known as the Black Watch, Liverpool Scottish Rifles, was made at a meeting at the George Hotel, Dale Street, on 15th November 1859. A volunteer corps was raised, known as the 19th Lancashire Rifle Volunteers, and this eventually comprised two Lowland companies (the 1st, under Captain James Maxwell and the 3rd, under Captain James M. Dowie) and one Highland company (the 2nd, under Captain G. A. Mackenzie). The Liverpool and London Chambers in Dale Street were used as a temporary headquarters, together with a storeroom in St. Domingo Barracks, until a house could be rented in Great George Square. The uniform was a grey tunic with red facings, trews in Urquhart tartan, and a Black Watch style of cap. The Government recognised the corps on 10th January 1860 as the 19th Lancashire Rifle Volunteer Corps (Liverpool Scottish Rifles), and a few days later, swearing in took place at Seel Street Police Station.

Almost immediately, disputes over the wearing of the kilt resulted in the mass resignation of the Highland company, which went on to form the Liverpool Highland Corps (71st Lancashire Rifle Volunteers). However, this did not end quarrels over dress. The committee introduced a grey kilt, similar to that worn by the London Scottish, and grey tunics with blue facings. This, however, resulted in the loss of those members who wanted a tartan, and under Captain Lamont, they formed Lamont's Highlanders, 2nd Liverpool Highland Company. This was never more than company strength and became the 3rd Company, the 79th Lancashire Volunteers but numbers declined and the unit was disbanded on 24th June 1863.

In 1860, a Scottish company was raised for the 1st Cheshire Rifle Volunteers. This was short-lived, again because of the issue of the kilt, which proved to be unacceptable to the Lord-Lieutenant of Cheshire; the company was disbanded, many of its members joining the 71st.

After an unsuccessful attempt by the 19th and 71st to re-unite, the 19th amalgamated with the Liverpool Rifle Brigade, as its Scottish company, whilst declining strength led to the 71st disbanding in 1864.

Despite these early difficulties, such early efforts kept alive a desire for a Scottish Battalion in Liverpool, which did eventually flourish at the time of the Boer War.

Efforts to form Scottish Battalions at the same time in Manchester (two Scottish companies of the 78th Lancashire Rifle Volunteers) and in Birmingham (a Scottish company of the 1st Warwickshire Rifle Volunteers) had no more lasting success, probably because of the Government's unwillingness to provide finance.

Apart from those mentioned above, it seems that the only other attempt to form Scottish Battalions in England was in 1914, when four battalions of the Tyneside Scottish were formed, as part of the Northumberland Fusiliers. They later became part of the Black Watch and subsequently an artillery unit [4].

The Boer War

Interest was revived by the Boer War. On 27th January 1900, a Mr. Milne (who was to become the first pipe major of the Liverpool Scottish) wrote to the local press, suggesting that 'the present crisis in South Africa offers a very favourable opportunity for raising a Liverpool Scottish Volunteer Corps'. A committee which included a number of eminent men, notably the Secretary of State for Scotland (Lord Balfour of Burleigh), the Lord Mayor of Liverpool, officers of the London Scottish, and several M.P.s, including Rt. Hon. Herbert Gladstone, was formed, a petition was forwarded to the War Office and authority was granted on 30th April.

In anticipation of the formation of the unit, Captain Christopher Forbes Bell was appointed commanding officer, with the rank of Lieutenant-Colonel, being joined by an adjutant, Captain John Cunynghame Robertson, formerly of the West India Regiment. Lt-Col. Forbes Bell was not to remain in command for long. On 26th July 1902, he resigned his commission owing to ill health, Major A. L. Macfie replacing him as Lieutenant-Colonel and commanding officer.

On 13th November, a meeting of all interested in the formation of the new Corps was held in Hope Hall (now the Everyman Theatre) and on 3rd December, the first Battalion Orders of the 8th (Scottish) Volunteer Battalion, the King's Liverpool Regiment announced that enrolment would commence the following day. On the first day, 80 men were processed and 60 accepted, only a fraction of the overwhelming number who presented themselves, and by the end of the year, the total strength had reached 200 [5]. There was an initial subscription of £2 and an annual subscription of 10 shillings, so that the recruits tended to be from middle-class backgrounds [6].

1901 was an eventful year. On 15th April, Highland dress including tartan was sanctioned. The tartan was based on that of the commanding officer - a slight variation of the Forbes tartan, omitting two of the narrow dark stripes[7]. However, the Government was not prepared to finance it and it had to be paid for by the men themselves. The badge adopted was that of the King's (the white horse of Hanover) superimposed on the Cross of St. Andrew. The first headquarters were in Highgate Street, Edge Hill and, although the building was still used until after the Second World War, the Liverpool Scottish soon moved into far larger premises in Fraser Street in the city centre (shown clearly on the 1906 1:2500 Ordnance Survey map).

By the beginning of June, the Battalion had Pipe and Bugle Bands, under Pipe-Major Milne (who sadly died in that month) and Drum-Major Sproul, a Signalling Class and Cycle Section and a Stretcher Bearers Section, under Surgeon-Captain Macalister, who had inaugurated a Department by the end of the year. The Battalion had no difficulty in finding a surgeon from amongst the many eminent Scots medics in Liverpool. Other events of 1901 were the first annual inspection on 27th July, at the old Exhibition Grounds in Edge Lane and the first annual rifle meeting at Altcar, where a standing camp had been established at the end of June. As early as February, Lieutenant J. A. Bingham became the first member of the Liverpool Scottish to volunteer for active service. It was necessary for members of Volunteer units to enlist in the regular army and he was seconded to the Imperial Yeomanry. Sadly he was also to be the first member of the Liverpool Scottish to be killed in action, at Klip River the following February[8]. In 1902, the Liverpool Scottish sent a service section of one officer and 21 other ranks to South Africa with the 1st Battalion, the Gordon Highlanders[9].

Up to the First World War, the Liverpool Scottish rose in strength (to 975 men in 1910) and pursued a very active programme. Annual events included the Inspection (in Wavertree Park or Sefton Park), the Rifle Meeting at Altcar, and the Prize Distribution in St. George's Hall which, from 1903, was followed by a Ball. The prizes were spoons carrying the Liverpool Scottish badge. Annual camps were held at various locations, including Knockaloe (Isle of Man), Stobs (near Hawick), Windmill Hill (Salisbury), Caerwys (Flintshire), Caton (near Lancaster) and Farleton (Carnforth). At these camps, the Liverpool Scottish was attached respectively to the 2nd Lothian Brigade, the South Lancashire Brigade and the West Lancashire Division.

The Liverpool Scottish was prominent in civic affairs, providing a Guard of Honour for Princess Louise's visit to Liverpool on 3rd March 1902 and for Lord Kitchener's visit on 11th October. On 19th July 1904, it paraded along Castle Street on the occasion of the King's visit for the laying of the foundation stone of the Anglican Cathedral. On 9th September 1905, it took part in the review and march past at the unveiling of the King's Memorial in St. John's Gardens. On 16th March 1906, it provided a Guard of Honour with pipers at the opening of the Northern Command Military Tournament at Tournament Hall, Edge Lane. Guards of Honour were also provided at the opening of the Scottish Home Industries Exhibition at the Philharmonic Hall on 26th November 1907 and, on 6th July 1909, at the King's departure from Knowsley, when he handed over colours presented by the Honorary Colonel, Lord Strathcona. On 18th September 1905, the Liverpool Scottish took part in the Royal Review, as part of the Scottish Volunteer Force (attached to the 2nd Lothian Brigade), on Edinburgh Castle Esplanade [10].

On 31st March 1908, the Volunteer Corps officially ceased to exist, the men having to re-enlist in the new Territorial Force, in which the Battalion was designated the 10th (Scottish) Battalion, King's (Liverpool) Regiment [11].

On 11th August 1911, the Liverpool Scottish arrival from annual camp, back at their barracks in Fraser Street, coincided with what was probably the worst riot in Liverpool's history. Tension had been building up for several days, because of a major transport strike, and police from various other forces had been brought in to the city. This culminated in the reading of the Riot Act and a baton charge by mounted police from Birmingham, to disperse a mass meeting of strikers in Lime Street, a few hundred yards from the barracks, where several wives and children of the soldiers were awaiting the return of the 'Scottish'. They were allowed to take shelter in the barracks until the danger was past [12].

The First World War

Along with other Territorial units, the Liverpool Scottish, which now totalled over 900 in all ranks, was mobilised at the outbreak of the First World War, the call going out to all members on 7th August 1914. Those who reported that day were quartered in the Shakespeare Theatre, across the road from the barracks in Fraser Street. The following day, when virtually all men had reported, 'G' and 'H' Companies remained in the Shakespeare, whilst 'A','B','C','D','E' and 'F' Companies were quartered nearby in the Stadium in Pudsey Street. In the early days of the war, some men were detailed to form working parties unloading vessels at the docks.

On 18th August, the Scottish left by train for training in Edinburgh, where they camped in King's Park, near Holyrood. From King's Park, Corporal George Carruthers wrote to his nine year old daughter Mollie, saying that he was 'longing to see the same old face that coaxed the sentries at the Stadium', a reference to an incident when she had charmed a sentry into bringing him briefly to the door. He added, 'I am A1. The discipline is very severe, so one has to be careful' - a realisation that 'Saturday soldiering' was over.

Before conscription was introduced in 1916, Territorials could be sent overseas only if they volunteered. All officers and 800 other ranks did volunteer and so were kept together as a unit, the remainder forming 'I' and 'K' Companies. On 10th October, they moved to the Dell, Tunbridge Wells and on 1st November, embarked at Southampton on the S.S. *Maidan* for Le Havre and final training at Blendecques, near St.Omer, with the 9th Infantry Brigade, 3rd Division. On 16th June 1915, at Belleward in the attack on Hooge, the Scottish took its own and much of the Brigade's objective but at a cost of 400 men.

The Scottish then joined the 55th Division, with other Lancashire units for the Battle of the Somme in August 1916. The losses in this battle are well known and the Scottish suffered in particular through an impossible objective - to save the remnants of the Liverpool Irish who had been cut off by the Germans; it was not realised that they had actually been captured the previous day. However, it was here that their medical officer, Captain Noel Chavasse, strictly of the R.A.M.C and incidentally son of the Bishop of Liverpool, was awarded his first Victoria Cross. At the third Battle of Ypres in 1917, the Scottish lost 55 killed and 180 wounded, including Captain Chavasse, who was killed but awarded the bar to the Victoria Cross posthumously. The Scottish took part in further actions at Epehy on St. Andrew's Day 1917 and, in early 1918, at Givenchy, where the 55th Division was the only British unit to hold the line intact.

As in other Scottish regiments, the pipers of the Liverpool Scottish played a significant role in leading the men into battle. Within the 1st Battalion, there were two Pipe-Majors, John Stoddart and John Stoddart Jr., Lance-Corporal John White, Sergeant E.J.Ogilvie, and Pipers James Rogers, John Graham, Thomas Wilson, Sydney Wilson, William Barclay and Charles Copland. In the 2nd Battalion, there were ten pipers, Thomas Wilson, James Gilfillan, Henry Forrester, Robert Johnson, Thomas Carlyle, Stanley Rae, Archibald Service, Don Fowler, James Martin, and Sydney Rogers. Many of them were wounded and John Stoddart (Sr.) was killed in July 1917 at Poperinghe. Others received bravery awards:

At Bois Grenier, Piper Thomas Wilson played his company over the top. Mostly, they were employed as stretcher bearers but in 1914, the pipers of 1st Battalion also served in the ranks. Piper Sydney Wilson was three times awarded the Certificate of Gallantry [13].

The second battalion had been raised in September 1914 and a third (reserve) battalion had been formed in 1915. The 2nd Battalion joined the 1st Battalion (seriously depleted by casualties after Givenchy, having already taken part in two raids in the Armentieres section [14]. The 3rd Battalion was responsible for recruitment and training and was camped at first in Weeton, near Blackpool, and as winter approached, were moved to more comfortable billets in St. Chads Road, South Shore, Blackpool (with officers billeted in the Belsfield Hotel) and later to Albert Road, North Shore (with officers in the Clifton Hotel). Corporal George Carruthers had not volunteered for overseas service and continued to send cards from 118 Albert Road to his family. In June 1916, they moved to Park, near Oswestry [15].

At the end of the war, the Liverpool Scottish had gained one double VC, 6 DSOs, 32 MCs, 20 DCMs, 133 MMs., and 67 mentions in dispatches, but had lost over 1100 men.

After the Armistice, the Scottish spent some months near Brussels and were later in charge of an embarkation camp at Antwerp [16]. The Scottish also had some involvement with the Irish 'Troubles' and, after the Easter Rising of 1916, provided escorts (mainly by returned overseas servicemen) for Irish prisoners being transported from Frongoch Camp, Bala, to Wormwood Scrubs and Wandsworth Prisons. Later, after the Armistice, 570 men were attached to the Argyll and Sutherland Highlanders, based at Kinsale [17].

After 1919

After the war, recruitment declined and, in 1920, the Liverpool Scottish was at half its pre-war strength. This was probably due to the general revulsion to war and to changes in the Territorial Army, which meant that bounties were lower and that members could now be ordered to serve overseas. By 1936, there were still vacancies for 130 men of 'at least partial Scots' descent' and the unit was still maintaining two of its individual traditions. All members paid an annual subscription and all officers had to serve a period in the ranks before receiving a commission.

In 1929, the Liverpool Scottish ended its links with the King's (Liverpool) Regiment for a time, when the Army List for June announced that it was to affiliate to and form part of the corps of the Queen's Own Cameron Highlanders and wear their badge. By 1st April 1938, the Scottish was almost at full strength, with 24 officers (4 short of its full establishment) and 706 other ranks (its full complement) [18].

In 1939, on the outbreak of the Second World War, a second battalion was raised. Throughout the War, the 1st Battalion was based in the UK, supplying men to other units and a platoon of volunteers went to Norway in 1940. The 2nd Battalion became the 89th Anti-Tank Regiment, Royal Artillery in 1942 and, after the war, the 1st Battalion served in Gibraltar from 1945 to 1947 [19].

In January 1947, the 1st Battalion was re-raised at their old headquarters in Fraser Street, with Lietenant-Colonel D. W. Renison as Commanding Officer and Captain J. M. Underwood as adjutant, as a motor battalion in the 23rd Armoured Brigade. The old 2nd Battalion re-formed as the 655th Light Anti-aircraft and Searchlight Regiment R.A. (Scottish) under Lietenant-Colonel A. H. M. Stewart.

In the immediate post-war years, the Scottish had quite a high profile on Merseyside. Its annual ball was resumed and its pipes and drums were often heard, especially at the annual church parade at St. Andrew's, Rodney Street where, in November 1948, a bronze war memorial was unveiled immediately below the 1914-1918 memorial. The week of the 21st-26th October 1950 was one of celebrations to mark the 50th anniversary of the Scottish, including a civic reception and dance and a civic dinner at the Town Hall [20]. The Scottish also moved into the recording studios, with the Pipes and Drums of the Battalion producing gramophone records on the Embassy label.

Meanwhile, the Liverpool Scottish Cadet Battalion, based at the original headquarters in Highgate Street, was flourishing with its own pipe band. In 1947, it camped at Cromarty, where its band played together with that of the 1st Inverness Cadet Battalion, Queen's Own Cameron Highlanders, who the following year camped at Stanley Park, Liverpool and made several appearances with their pipes, drums and highland dancers at the Tower Ballroom, New Brighton and on the Promenade [21].

As a result of reorganisation of the Territorial Army in 1956, the Scottish reverted to its old infantry role, as part of the 125th Infantry Brigade in the 42nd (South Lancashire) Division [22].

In 1967, the Liverpool Scottish moved from its Fraser Street headquarters to a former Royal Signals H.Q. - Signal House, which was then re-named Forbes House - in Score Lane, Childwall. It again became a prominent landmark on Queens Drive (the main Liverpool ring Road) until 1999 when the Liverpool Scottish (now reduced in strength to two platoons) moved to Townsend Lane as part of the Kings Cheshire Regiment. The keystone with the insignia is to be moved to a site at Belleward, Hooge, the scene of the Great War battle.

A new memorial stone is to be placed in St John's Garden, replacing the original which will be moved to be the Scottish Wood which is to be created between K and M ranges at Altcar.

A pipe band is now supplied by the Liverpool Scottish Association, whose members need not be members of the Liverpool Scottish. It is frequently seen in the Childwall area, not only at the headquarters of the Scottish but also those of the neighbouring Royal Naval Association.

Conclusion

The establishment of the Liverpool Scottish reflects both the Scottish regimental and military tradition, stretching back over many centuries but operating within the British army after 1745, and the growth of the 'volunteer army' in Victorian times, particularly following the Crimean War. There were only a very few cities outwith London where regiments based on in-migrant groups (Scots, Welsh and Irish) could realistically be established and in the event, only in Newcastle and Liverpool were Scottish regiments founded successfully.

The regiment was probably most significant in the period from the 1910s to the 1940s, including the two World Wars. Its decline in recent years reflects not only army reorganisation but also the declining numbers of Scots on Merseyside, which made it increasingly difficult for the regiment to maintain a specific Scottish identity.

References

1. L. Colley (1994), <u>Britons. Forging the Nation 1707-1837</u>, Pimlico: London, p.120
2. C. Harvie (1994), <u>Scotland and Nationalism. Scottish Society and Politics 1707-1994</u>, Routledge: London, p.61

3. Ibid
4. Dennis Reeves (1972), "Liverpool Rifle Volunteers 1859", Military Historical Bulletin, vol. XXII no. 87, February.
5. 'Historical Records', Liverpool Scottish Regimental Gazette, December 1912, pp.3-5.
6. Peter Howell Williams (1971), Liverpolitana, p.21.
7. Frank Adam (1908), The Clans, Septs and Regiments of the Scottish Highlands, p.421.
8. 'Hist. Records' (op.cit.), pp.4-6.
9. The Liverpolitan, March 1936, p.25 and May 1938, p.18.
10. 'Hist. Records' (op.cit.), pp.6-17.
11. Ibid., p.14.
12. (i) An Everyday History of Liverpool (1911), vol. II.
    (ii) H.R.Hikins (1961), 'The Liverpool General Transport Strike 1911', Transactions of the Historic Society of Lancashire and Cheshire, vol. 113, pp.169-195.
    (iii) Oral account of eye-witness, Mrs.M.I.Munro.
13. Brevet-Col. Sir Bruce Seton and Pipe-Major John Grant (1920), The Pipes of War. A Record of the Achievements of Pipers of Scottish and Overseas Regiments during the War 1914-1918, Maclehose Jackson, Glasgow.
14. (i) The Liverpolitan, March 1936 and May 1938, op.cit.
    (ii) A.M. McGilchrist (1930), The Liverpool Scottish 1900-1919, pp.13-18.
15. Ibid., p. 259
16. Historical Records of the Queen's Own Cameron Highlanders, 1952-62, vol.iv, p.456.
17. McGilchrist, Op. cit., pp. 263-264.
18. (i) The Liverpolitan, March 1936 and May 1938, op.cit.
    (ii) Hist.Records,Q.O.C.H., p.456
19. R. Westlake (1986), The Territorial Battalions - A Pictorial History, 1859-1985.
20. Hist. Records, Q.O.C.H., vol.vii, pp.38-39.
21. Ibid., vol.iv, p.456.
22. Ibid., vol.vii, p.41.

The Liverpool Scottish at Caton Camp in 1910

The Liverpool Scottish in King's Park, Edinburgh immediately after mobilisation in
August 1914

Spoons awarded annually by the Liverpool Scottish as individual prizes
for shooting and other competitions

Men of the 3rd Battalion (who did <u>not</u> volunteer for overseas services)
outside their billet at 118 Albert Road Blackpool

118 Albert Road Blackpool today

The H.Q. from 1911 to 1967 is now Pickwick's Club

Forbes House, Score Lane, Childwall. Until recently the H.Q. of the Liverpool Scottish

The Programme of the Annual Ball in 1930 was probably typical. It commenced with the Grand March, accompanied by pipers who also played for the Eightsome Reel, Foursome Reel and Highland Scottish. There was an exhibition of Highland Dancing but the rest of the programme was not particularly Scottish, consisting mainly of waltzes and foxtrots to the music of Bonners Orchestra. However the Lancers was performed twice, one to a medley of Burns' tunes and the other to Harry Lauder's songs

The Liverpool Scottish memorial stone in a secluded part of
St John's Gardens is easily missed

CHAPTER SEVEN

Social Life and Charitable Effort

Introduction

It has been said that, where there are two Scots, they form a Caledonian Society and certainly, the Scots who emigrated were often very active in establishing social clubs and Highland Games and maintaining traditional festivities. In America, for example, Donaldson refers not only to the maintenance of traditional festivities at Hogmanay and Hallowe'en but how St. Andrew's Day was celebrated in the New World when it had been all but forgotten at home. By the mid-nineteenth century, there were numerous Burns Clubs across America and in 1836, the Highland Society of New York held its first Highland Games[1].

Such expressions of affinity with the 'homeland' are, of course, relatively common, amongst all immigrant communities and the Scots overseas reacted in a way reminiscent, for example, of Asians in Britain today. Social clubs and community gatherings of this sort have a great importance in allowing people of a common heritage to come together and to renew friendships and memories. As Hunter neatly points out, in relation to the Scots of Glengarry County in eastern Ontario,

> It is a simple matter to make fun of the enormous pomp and ceremony surrounding events like the Glengarry Highland Games.........But to adopt such an attitude is simply to demonstrate one's own failure to comprehend the distinction between symbol and substance. What is being celebrated at the Glengarry Highland Games and similar festivals is the profound sense of community generated over the last two hundred years in the homesteads and the villages established with such difficulty in this little bit of North America.........what matters........is the opportunity which such an event provides each year for many thousands of men and women......to renew their acquaintance with the place which, for several generations, their people have called home[2].

It may be that distance lends a certain enchantment to this concept of 'home' and certainly expatriates in America and Australia have managed to maintain their traditions over a number of generations. But even in England, where expatriate Scots are perhaps less likely to adopt such a rosy view of their homeland, Scottish clubs and societies are of great social significance.

Early Scots Charities

The first known societies on Merseyside were formed in the late nineteenth century, although it is certain that Scots were meeting for social events a hundred years earlier. It has already been seen (in Chapter Three) that the proposal to build the first Scots' Kirk in Liverpool was made at a St. Andrew's dinner in 1792[3]. It is also known that, on the 25th January 1859, the centenary of Robert Burns's birth was celebrated in the old Philharmonic Hall, Liverpool, with the 'haggis duly graced' and then distributed to a crowded hall, and that this gathering then seems to have been held annually in the Conservative Club in Dale Street (now the Municipal Annexe)[4].

The oldest society on Merseyside and, indeed in the north west of England, is the Liverpool Caledonian Association, which was formed for charitable purposes in 1869 - to give relief in Liverpool and District to Scots or those of Scottish descent, who from sickness or other cause needed assistance. Little is known of its early work except through references in local directories but its relief committee met twice weekly (Tuesdays and Fridays at 4.00 p.m.) in its offices, at 13 Drury Buildings, 21-23 Water Street, to consider applications for regular and casual payments. An article in *The Liverpolitan* described its work in 1937:

> Permanent grants are given to aged people under 70 years of age, whilst some in receipt of old age pensions are, in special circumstances, assisted weekly. The sick are provided with invalid food and, when fit for admission, are sent to convalescent homes or sanatoria. Persons stranded in Liverpool are taken in hand and restored to their friends in Scotland, and assistance is afforded in many other ways, special regard being paid to ex-servicemen.

It raised money, largely through subscriptions. In 1937, donors of ten guineas became Life Members, whilst ordinary members paid one guinea. Membership was also open to firms (the senior staff member being entered as a member of the Association), whilst any minister who preached a sermon which raised ten guineas also became a life member[5].

Gore's Directory for 1908 lists its officers and indicates that it had impressive support amongst the merchants and medics of Merseyside and of Liverpool:

President: The Duke of Connaught and Strathearn
Chairman: Alex Guthrie (merchant with Balfour and Williamson)
Chairman (Relief Committee): Hugh Frame (tailor)
Hon. Treasurer: Richard Henderson (Managing Director, Anchor Line)
Hon. Secretary: W. Leitch (marine insurance broker)
Hon. Chaplain: Rev. James Hamilton, St. Andrew's Church of Scotland,
Rodney Street
Hon. Physicians: David Smart, E. Harris, Alex Craigmile, R. Gordon
Smith, George Johnson
Hon. Surgeon: George Gibson Hamilton (practising in Rodney Street)[6]

Another Liverpool charity, largely supported by Scots, was the Liverpool Sheltering Homes (already referred to in Chapter Five). This was largely due to the work of Louisa Birt, a member of the congregation at Fairfield Presbyterian Church, with considerable support from her minister, Rev. R. H. Lundie and his wife. Born in Campsie, Stirlingshire, the Macpherson sisters, Annie Parlane, Rachel and Louisa Caroline, became interested in the ideas of Froebel, the German educationalist, and opened a home for destitute children in East London. They arranged a new life for many of these children in Canada - a fashionable idea at the time - and opened a number of new homes over there too [7].

Louisa frequently passed through Liverpool en route between London and Canada and was appalled at the poverty which she saw there. In November 1872, at the invitation of Mr. Alexander Balfour, a Liverpool Scots businessman and philanthropist, her sister, Annie Macpherson, addressed a public meeting in the town and the following year, the first Liverpool Sheltering Home opened in Byrom Hall, Byrom Street, in one of the town's poorest districts, just north of the town centre. The premises were provided rent-free by one of Mrs. Birt's many well-wishers and, from 1878, Mrs. Birt came to live there herself. The home always tried to provide an excellent Christmas dinner for all the poor children of the area and, from 1885, the local council allowed the free use of St. George's Hall for the event. Around 1883, a Sheltering Home for girls was established in Sugnall Street (by St. George's Church)[8]. In 1884, land in Myrtle Street adjacent to the girls' home was acquired and a new home was built to replace the Byrom Street premises, which were in very poor condition [9].

An advertisement for the Sheltering Homes in 1908 stated:

over 200 fresh children are received each year. Over 180 emigrate yearly and are placed in comfortable homes with Canadian families of good standing and repute.

Boys between 10 and 12 and girls between 4 and 16 were accepted for the homes and:

> in addition to ordinary school instruction, the girls have cooking, laundry and 'cutting out' lessons, while the boys have carpentry classes and training in the management of horses and cattle.
> A donation of £12 would defray the cost of emigration for one child [10].

There was never any religious discrimination in helping destitute children though, sadly, that gave rise to accusations of using the homes to subvert Roman Catholic children [11].

Scottish Social Societies

The first Scottish social society formed on Merseyside was the Liverpool and District St. Andrew Society, founded in 1890. This started originally as a pipe band, which diversified its activities to include both social evenings and outdoor activities such as rambles. Little is known of its early history, as its first existing minute book dates from 1909. For much of its life, it met in the church hall of Fairfield Presbyterian Church.

Rule 2 of the Society states its objects as:

> the cultivation and maintenance of Scottish sentiment; the study of Scottish History; the fostering of Scottish song; the celebration of national anniversaries; the promotion of social intercourse amongst the Scottish people resident in and around the city.

Rule 3 states that full members must be Scots by birth, marriage or descent. Persons with no such connection may enrol as associate members and cannot serve in any executive position [12].

The second society in the area was the Liverpool North End and District Scottish Association, founded in Bootle in 1896. Birkenhead and District St. Andrew Society was formed in 1918, St. Helens and District Caledonian Society in 1922, the Liverpool Burns Club in 1924, the Liverpool Scots' Association in 1925, the Liverpool Scots Society in 1926 and Wallasey Caledonian Society in 1932 [13].

The Liverpool Burns Club seems to have developed from a group who had been meeting annually since 1859, until it was suggested that they might meet more frequently and include socials, rambles and lectures on Scottish subjects in their programme. At first they were known as the Robert Burns Society, changing the name when the society affiliated to the Burns Federation [14].

It is surprising that no society was formed in Birkenhead before 1918, as Scots had always had such an influence on the town. Indeed, it was probably the strength of Scots sentiment in the town which resulted in the tremendous popularity of an unknown performer who sang a repertoire of Scottish songs at the Argyle Theatre. It is generally thought that the fame of Harry Lauder dated from his first appearance at this theatre on 3rd January 1898, for a fee of £4 per week [15].

The inaugural meeting of the Birkenhead and District St. Andrew Society was convened on 9th December 1918, with typical Scottish caution, 'to discuss the advisability of inaugurating a Birkenhead Scottish Society'. However, it was agreed to form such a society, to be known as the 'Birkenhead St. Andrew's Society'. The proposer was then asked to read out the objects and rules of the original St. Andrew's Society. What this means is unclear, as there is no record of a previous St. Andrew's Society in Birkenhead but, presumably it was intended to model it on some other society - possibly one in Scotland [16]. The objects were (and still are):

> 2(a) To promote homely gatherings in true Scottish fashion, where Song and Dance can be enjoyed in a happy and friendly association. (b) To keep alive the matchless Songs of Scotland and preserve the traditional dances. (c) To provide a welcome home from home with the real Scottish atmosphere so congenial to all those of Scottish birth, ancestry or family connections who love the land of Scotia.
>
> 3 The Society shall be non-political, non-sectarian and interdenominational [17].

Mr. Alex McKechnie (an insurance director) was elected as the society's first president, with Messrs. John Wilson and John Bradshaw as vice-presidents, Mr. Stewart Cruden as treasurer, Miss Susan Bradshaw as secretary, and Miss Marion White as her assistant, together with a committee of four ladies and four gentlemen. Rev. J. Faichney (Minister of Hamilton Memorial Presbyterian Church) was Chaplain.

The first meeting was a musical evening, attended by '66 members and a few friends', who were entertained by Miss Alice Johnston (Highland dancer), Mr. Will Gardner (piper), Masters McDougall (instrumentalists) and Mr. David Boyd (elocutionist). On 1st April 1919, a meeting was held in Boilermakers' Hall, Argyle Street, at which Rev. J. Faichney delivered a lecture on 'Baroness Nairne - Her Life and Works', followed by a musical programme of choir and soloists.

On St. Andrew's Day 1919, a service was held at Hamilton Memorial Church, conducted by Rev. Faichney, and concluding with 'the singing of the psalms in the old Scottish fashion', which was deemed to be very enjoyable. On 4th December in the same year, Major Archer of Liverpool gave a lecture on the theme 'Through Scotland with Sir Walter Scott'. This was described as a 'limelight' (i.e. magic lantern lecture).

The main summer activity was an annual picnic at Raby Mere, a local beauty spot, at which the society arrived by charabanc. Liverpool and District St. Andrew's Society members were invited to join them and attendances of about 200 were common. It seems that many of the society's earliest members were employed in shipbuilding or marine engineering (several originating in the Greenock area) and this probably accounts for the Society's early use of Boilermakers' Hall [18].

The Liverpool Scots Society also had an informal origin. A group of Scots, who had met weekly in a hall in Shaw Street to enjoy traditional dances, decided to organise themselves on a more formal basis and formed the Society, which met in the Conservative Club in Durning Road, Edge Hill [19]. Unlike most Scots' societies, they had access to a licensed bar where some interesting debates took place, as many of the Liverpool Scots were active Labour Party supporters [20].

Minute books for the first ten years of the St. Helens and District Caledonian Society have been lost but that for 1932 gives a good picture of its activities, which included a regular dancing class; a New Year Party, consisting of a whist drive and dance costing 2/6; a St. Andrew's Night lantern lecture on 'Primitive Life in the Highlands'; a Burns Dinner at a local hotel costing 3/6; and a dramatic society and concert party which put on an annual show.

From the beginning, benevolence played a major part in the Society's activities and the grants and gifts listed in the first existing minute book indicate that the Society played an active role in the life of St. Helens. They include:

£1.1/- to purchase a corset for the crippled daughter of a poor family in the town;

10/6 to the St. Helens Poor Children's Holiday appeal;

£1.1/- to the annual Poor Children's Christmas Party;

5/- and 1/- respectively to two poor Scots travelling through the town;

£21 to the St. Helens and District Nursing Association to furnish a bedroom in the Nursing Association Building;

£5 to the Y.M.C.A towards a new Boys Club building (presented in person by the President's wife to Princess Helena Victoria on her visit to St. Helens)

£1.1/- was also donated to the refurbishment of the Burns Mausoleum [21].

Establishing a Federation

By 1927, there were many similar societies throughout Lancashire and Cheshire and there were proposals to unite them in a Lancashire and Cheshire Federation of Scottish Societies. On 4th March 1927, a meeting was called at the County Council offices in Preston by a Mr. George Drysdale, at which ten societies were represented and there were many apologies from other interested societies. The formation of a federation was agreed in principle and this was confirmed at a second meeting at the Lion Hotel, Warrington, on 30th April. This meeting was followed by tea and a concert, presented by Warrington Caledonian Society.

The ten original member societies included three from Merseyside, namely Birkenhead St. Andrew, Liverpool Scots Society and St. Helens and District Caledonian. At the third meeting, on 10th September at the Central Library, Blackpool, Liverpool and District St. Andrew was also admitted. A practical outcome of this meeting was an agreement to compile a list of speakers and singers for Burns Dinners. After the meeting, they were entertained to tea and a concert, by the Mayor of Blackpool.

In the early years of the Federation, attempts to introduce Scottish cultural activities met with limited success. At a meeting in December 1928, it was agreed to co-operate with Morecambe Corporation in organising a Highland Games, which was held on 17th July 1929; the Duke of Atholl was Chieftain of the Games. Entry to some events was reserved for Federation members only. A singing competition for boys and girls connected with the federated societies was held, in conjunction with the Wallasey Musical Festival in October 1930, but attracted very few entries. Attempts to establish an essay competition for under-16s in 1929 had little more success, possibly because of the rather unimaginative subjects - 'The Character of Rob Roy as depicted by Sir Walter Scott' in the first year and 'The Scot as an Empire Builder' in the second. In the third, it was recognised that these titles might have been too difficult and the more straightforward 'Bonnie Prince Charlie' was set. An adult competition was introduced too, the set piece being 'The Life and Work of Sir Walter Scott'. Bowls and golf competitions were also introduced about the same time but they too met with a poor response. Rather more successful was the idea of making the Annual General Meeting into a weekend conference, the first being held in Southport in June 1931, at which the Federation delegates were entertained to a Civic Supper Dance on the Friday evening and invited the Mayor to their own Supper Dance the following evening; they organised a Highland Games, jointly with Southport Corporation, on the Saturday [22].

During the inter-war years, a number of Scottish and 'Anglo-Scottish' concerts were held. At first they were largely due to the initiative of the Liverpool and District St. Andrew's Society, whose own dancing octette would entertain. The concerts were organised by one of its members, Wullie Sutherland, whose own act was a Harry Lauder impersonation; he was a very small man - of similar stature to Lauder himself. Other entertainers who frequently appeared at these concerts and at various societies' dinners included Alex McKelvie (tenor), a policeman by profession, Will Gardner (piper), Norman Stewart (piper) and his daughter, Jean (Highland dancer), Mollie Carruthers (pianist) and her sister Jean (mezzo-soprano). It seems that this concert party was prepared to give its services to other organisations, as for example, a concert was given for the Parish Church of St. Philip's, Shiel Road on 16th November 1934 [23]. Other performers in the later 1930s included dancers Ruby Jamieson and Bessie Carruthers, younger sister of Mollie and Jean.

Other Scots Organisations

During this period, there were Scottish societies on Merseyside, which were not affiliated to the Lancashire and Cheshire Federation and which were somewhat different in character. When the *Liverpool Echo* quoted Mr.Hamish Rae, secretary of the Burns Club as saying that the 'Scottish clubs in the city were mainly dance societies', this provoked an angry reply from Mr. Samuel Munro, secretary of the Wallace Society of Liverpool, pointing out that his own society was a national one, where 'we discuss questions on every phase of Scottish National life - social, religious, political, industrial and, when necessary, religious' [24]. The Wallace Society may have been formed after a dispute in the Burns Club, of which Samuel Munro had once been secretary and it seems to have been relatively short-lived. Programmes for its annual Burns Dinners exist from 1927 to 1933 and give some indication of its distinctiveness. Whilst the other societies were non-political, the Wallace Society seems to have shown definite Scottish Nationalist sympathies. Unlike other societies, there was no Loyal Toast, the main toast being to 'Scotland: A Nation' (or 'Scotland Yet'), with a further toast to 'Our Celtic Kinsfolk'. Replies were given by individuals with such Nationalist credentials as Councillor David Logan (later MP for the Scotland Division of Liverpool and leader of the Irish Nationalist Party), F. B. Fitzpatrick, JP, of the same party, J. Fitzsimmons, secretary of Liverpool University Irish Society, J. H. Jones, editor of *Y Brython*, J. H. Davies (Plaid Cymru) and Rev. D. Francis Roberts, minister of the Welsh Calvinistic Methodist Church in Everton.

Notable speakers at other dinners included Rev. William Paxton, FRGS, FSA (Scot.), minister of Great George Street Congregationalist Church and one of the city's most notable preachers, and Matthew Anderson, a person of some importance in the city as head of the Liverpool Organisation Ltd. This body had been set up in 1923 by local businessmen, to advance the interests of Merseyside, by encouraging businesses to move into the area and by staging events to project the city's image, such as an annual Civic Week. It was established as a limited company in 1928 and funded with subscriptions from over three hundred companies and grants from the Corporations of Liverpool, Birkenhead, Bootle and Wallasey. Matthew Anderson was largely responsible for the Liverpool and Manchester Railway Centenary celebrations in 1930, as a result of which his organisation was invited to put on similar pageants for other towns (including Ayr).

The high point of the Wallace Society's existence was probably its 1931 Burns Dinner, when the toast to the Immortal Memory of Robert Burns was given by no less a person than Christopher Murray Grieve (the poet Hugh MacDiarmid), who lived in Liverpool for about a year. He began working as publicity officer for the Liverpool Organisation on 12th May 1930, writing articles on shipping and other matters for various periodicals. His wife, Peggy, did not come with him, became pregnant by a Breton nationalist called la Rue, and had an (illegal) abortion. It was during his time in Liverpool that MacDiarmid's marriage finally ended. He began drinking more heavily than usual and lost his job after about a year. However, it was in Liverpool that he did much of his work on one of his great poems - 'To Circumjack Cencrastus' [25].

About 1929, graduates of Edinburgh University formed their own club in Liverpool and former pupils of George Heriot's School, Edinburgh, now resident in Liverpool, set up the Liverpool Heriot Club and considered extending membership to all former pupils of Scottish schools now living in the area. At a meeting held at the Angel Hotel, Dale Street, in December 1930, the Heriot Club agreed to sponsor a Scottish Former Pupils' Club, its first proposed activity to be an excursion to Edinburgh for the Scotland - England Rugby match [26]. The fact that three societies with such exclusive membership were considered viable gives some indication of the number of exiled Scots on Merseyside at the time.

Another indication of the numerical strength of Scots on Merseyside is provided by the fact that, in 1937, the Winter Gardens Theatre in New Brighton issued vouchers, which offered special concessions to all members of Caledonian and Burns Societies for the opening night (Monday 8th March) of the Scottish play, 'Marigold', by L. Allen Harker and F. R. Pryor, 'direct from the Royalty Theatre, London, after 750 performances'. This received a generally good review from the *Liverpool Echo*'s dramatic critic. Under the heading, 'Marigold delights at the Winter Gardens', he praised the set, costumes and acting, although the plot was simplistic and often unbelievable. Set in 1842, Marigold (played by Katharine Page), an innocent teenager from a manse near Edinburgh, is rescued from an arranged marriage with a much older laird, by Mrs. Pringle (the farewell appearance of Jean Clyde) to marry her soldier suitor [27].

Scots were also active in sport and their numbers led to proposals to form a Liverpool Scots' Sports Club in 1934, under the title of Liverpool Caledonians. The main mover behind the scheme was Andrew Sim, an Aberdonian and amateur footballer with the West Kirby club. Writing to the *Liverpool Echo,* he described his ideas:

> There are 30,000 of the clan on Merseyside and, properly organised, they should make a fine sporting body. We have nothing of the calibre of London Caledonians; no rugby team similar to London Scottish; in fact Liverpool does not offer facilities to Scottish sportsmen.

> There are possibilities of this being remedied; a group of enthusiastic Scots being hopeful of forming a first class football team to compete with the best of Merseyside amateur sides and in time, perhaps with the best of London and the rest of Britain.......[28].

London Caledonians at this time, played in the Isthmian League.

A Committee was formed in July 1934 and, interestingly, the formation of the Liverpool Caledonians coincided with the launch of a 'Young Wales' team which later became Liverpool Welsh. The President of the club was Matthew Anderson of the Liverpool Organisation (described above) and the Chairman was a Mr. W. Nelson. Players included Don Farmer of Marine F.C., A.C. McLeod and Andrew Sim of West Kirby and the three sons of Alec Raisbeck, a former Liverpool half-back and former Scottish internationalist. The long term aim was to become active in various sports but, unsurprisingly, they began with football, entering a team in both the Liverpool Challenge Cup and Liverpool Amateur Cup in 1934-35. The team played a number of friendlies over the next three or four years and entered cup competitions but it is not clear if they played regularly in a local league. The plan to move into other sports was frustrated by the onset of the War, although the Caledonians did play American rules baseball for some years in the late 1940s. Continued interest was probably assured by the United States forces presence at nearby Burtonwood.

The Second World War and After

Most activities were halted by the Second World War. The Liverpool Scots' Society's meetings were brought to an abrupt end, when their meeting place was damaged in an air raid on 28th November 1940. The adjacent Technical College was destroyed with the accompanying deaths of 180 people who were sheltering in its cellars; it is believed to have been the worst civilian incident of the war [29]. Meanwhile, the Lancashire and Cheshire Federation held no meetings at all during the war years [30].

However, the desire to return to normal, as soon as possible after the war, was epitomised by the Liverpool Scots Society, who began to meet in their old venue, despite the fact that one wall was being replaced and their only protection from the great freeze and power cuts of early 1947 was a plastic sheet and their only defence against dust and dirt was their vice president, Mr. William Faulds, who personally brushed out the hall before each meeting [31].

The Lancashire and Cheshire Federation met again, in Liverpool, in October 1946, and now became more active than ever before. In the immediate post war years, several new societies were formed on Merseyside, including Crosby Caledonian Society (1947), West Derby Caledonian Society (1947), Southport Scottish

Association (1952), Deeside Caledonian Society (1955) and Maghull and District Scottish Society (1963). Other societies formed in this period but no longer in existence were Wirral Scottish Society (c1947), The Highland Society of Liverpool (1950) and Moreton and District Caledonian Association (c.1953). To some extent, the location of these societies reflects the general movement of population to newer residential areas around Liverpool and the Wirral [32].

Many of the annual events which the Federation had tried to organise in the inter-war years, with varying success, now became firmly established features. On 7th April 1951, the first Musical Festival was held at St. John's Presbyterian Church Hall, Warrington, with competitions in singing, Scottish Country Dancing and elocution. It was followed by an evening concert, at which the winners were invited to perform with other artistes. In future years, the scope was extended to include public speaking, essay, instrumentalist, craft and cookery sections and the event was held at venues throughout the Federation's area, though very frequently in North Merseyside (or South Sefton as it is now known) [33].

The same year saw the first of the annual Highland Games (known at first as a Field Day) at Crawford's Sports Ground, Wavertree, Liverpool on 14th July. After using various other venues, the Games were held at Stanley Park, Blackpool in 1962 and, apart from a four year break (1974-1977), when they were held in the Greater Manchester area, they have been held there every year. Its pipe band competition became particularly popular, after the Federation affiliated to the Scottish Pipe Bands Association in 1962.

The Federation's AGM developed into a weekend residential conference, with a Civic Reception on the Friday evening, a Dinner and Ball on the Saturday evening and church service on the Sunday morning. At first it was held in various towns, but Fleetwood's civic hospitality was so impressive that, since 1962, it has been held nowhere else [34].

Meanwhile, the Merseyside sub-section of the Federation was returning to its pre-war activity, directed by Mr. Wullie Sutherland (referred to above). A highlight of the concert held on 18th February 1952 in the Picton Hall, Liverpool, was the personal appearance of the Liverpool F.C and Scottish international footballer, Mr. Billy Liddell [35]. The other annual Merseyside event was a Highland Ball, held for many years at New Brighton Tower Ballroom. In 1957, music was provided by no less a band than Jimmy Shand's. The Tower was eventually demolished but the event continued for several years at the Grafton Rooms in Liverpool.

For many years, one of the most prominent men on the Scottish scene was Bobbie Anderson. Son of the founder of one of the earliest Scots societies on Merseyside, his many talents included Highland dancing, which he taught, and singing, particular Harry Lauder's songs. He was a member of several societies and was Chieftain of the Federation for many years, ensuring communication between the member societies through a quarterly newsletter and through his work for its annual events. He was held in particular esteem in Fleetwood, where the Federation conference was held, the Mayor and Mayoress of Wyre attending his funeral in 1984. He was an elder of St. Andrew's Presbyterian Church, Waterloo and a captain of the 42nd Liverpool B.B. company at the Union Presbyterian Church, Kirkdale.

The Federation's main charitable effort, a scholarship fund, had been set up in 1937 and, in 1948, it became known as the Student Aid Fund and grants were made to children of members of any affiliated society in need of help with their education. By 1972, it was felt that it had outlived its usefulness and was wound up. (This was a time when most students with reasonably frugal tastes could survive on their grants)[36].

Like most cities, Liverpool has had a number of pipe bands. Pipe-Major Angus Macleod founded the Clan Macleod Pipe Band, whose Annual Highland Ball was held in the magnificent setting of St. George's Hall, from the end of the Second World War to the 1960s. The spectacle of dancers and pipers made it annually one of Liverpool's major social events, and the galleries were crowded with spectators [37].

Another gentleman who contributed enormously to piping on Merseyside was Tom Graham, who learned piping with the 1st Battalion, the Argyll and Sutherland Highlanders and, after demobilisation, worked briefly in the mines in Fife and played with the Cowdenbeath Public Pipe Band. He then came to Merseyside, where he was first associated with the Bootle Village Pipe Band (founded by Mr Tom Shacklady) and then with the Liverpool Scottish pipe band. In the late 1960s, he was invited to teach a new pipe band, formed by 103 Light Air Defence Regiment, Royal Artillery (TA), whose kilts were provided by Brigadier Douglas Crawford, of Crawford's Biscuits.

In 1949, Tom Graham married a piper and together they had seven children, all of whom took an interest in the pipes or drums; unsurprisingly, the family was able to form the basis of the Graham Highland Pipers in the early 1970s. In 1976, Liverpool City Council gave permission for the band to use the title 'City of Liverpool Pipe

Band'. As members of the family left Merseyside, the band unfortunately broke up but Tom Graham's influence continued as a teacher of the pipes in further education classes. One of Tom Graham's pupils, Kevin Monaghan, formed the Piob Mhor Pipe Band in Norris Green. The Graham Highland Pipers practised in the hall of Stuart Road Baptist Church and trained a pipe band for the church's Boys Brigade Company (the 67th Liverpool) [38].

Across the Mersey, the 1st Moreton Boys Brigade Company, based at Moreton Methodist Church, once had a very successful pipe band, founded by Roy Gordon and which wore the Gordon tartan. Its instructor, Ted Humphries, also formed the Wallasey (later Wirral) Pipe Band and there were always close links between the two bands. When the 1st Moreton's band disbanded, its remaining members joined the Wirral Pipe Band [39].

Other Boys Brigade companies which have had pipe bands at different times have been the 14th Liverpool (at Princes Road Presbyterian Church), the 23rd Liverpool (at Holy Trinity, Walton Breck Road), the 45th Liverpool (at Stoneycroft Methodist Church) [40], and the 5th St. Helens (at Christ Church, Eccleston) [41].

The Clan Wallace Pipe Band originated as the Balmoral Pipe Band in 1949. It was later known as the Victory Pipe Band and, in August 1979, adopted its present name because the members thought the Wallace tartan particularly attractive! For a time its pipe-major was a postman, Harold Cook, who also formed a Post Office Pipe Band. Although it was short-lived, it was the only Post Office pipe band south of the border [42].

Conclusion

The tendency for minority groups to self-segregate within cities is well known. Minorities may cluster together as a function of internal group cohesiveness, as a means of providing mutual support, as a defence or in order to preserve their own cultures. Black minority groups, for example, who have frequently suffered discrimination and harassment, often cluster in well defined areas for reasons of defence and mutual support.

The Scots, as not only a white minority, but a 'British' minority within a part of 'Britain', are clearly in rather a different position and it has been shown that, unlike for example the Irish, the Scots have not become especially segregated. Because of this, Scottish societies and organisations, operating throughout the area, have been important as the mechanisms by which 'Scottishness' has been preserved, and such organisations have allowed Scots to meet and to support each other. The range of Scottish organisations - social, musical and sporting - is extensive, reflecting the size of the Scottish community on Merseyside in previous years. The Second World War led to the cessation of some activities and it is to be expected that, as the community becomes more distant from its roots, other activities will also cease. Nevertheless, the tenacity of Scots in many corners of the world, to maintain their societies, institutions and traditions, suggests that a core of activity is likely to remain on Merseyside for generations to come.

References

1. G. Donaldson (1966), The Scots Overseas, Robert Hale, London, pp.124-5
2. J. Hunter, A Dance Called America. The Scottish Highlands, the United States and Canada, Mainstream, Edinburgh, pp.86-7
3. St. Andrew's Kirk, Rodney Street, Unpublished paper.
4. The Liverpolitan, January 1937.
5. Ibid., March 1937. Article on 'Scottish Charity on Merseyside'.
6. Gore's Liverpool Directory, 1908.
7. 'Louisa Birt - Children's Home Founder', Liverpool Citizen, 14th January 1888, p.3.
8. Liverpol Citizen, p.163.
9. Ibid., p.154.
10. Gore's Liverpool Directory, 1908, p.2263.
11. The Porcupine, 2nd December 1892.
12. Syllabus 1989-1990, Liverpool and District St. Andrew Society.
13. Information provided by Mr. George Penman.
14. Information provided by Mrs. Hazel Bishop.
15. Carol E. Bidston (1985), Birkenhead of Yesteryear, p.18.
16. Birkenhead and District St. Andrew's Society, Minute Book.
17. Ibid., membership card.
18. Ibid., Minute Book.
19. Liverpool Scots Society: short history in 21st anniversary dinner programme, 1947.
20. Personal memory - S.A.Munro.
21. Information provided by Mrs. E. Adam (St. Helens).

22. Lancashire and Cheshire Federation of Scottish Societies, 1927-1977 (50th Anniversary brochure).

23. Menus of annual dinners - Robert Burns Club 1926; Liverpool Scots Society 1929; Programme, Liverpool and District St. Andrew Society Concert, 30th March 1930; Programme, Anglo-Scots Concert, 16 November 1934.

24. Liverpool Echo, 19th December 1930.

25. Wallace Society menus of annual dinners 1927, 1929, 1931, 1932, 1933; Hugh MacDiarmid (1972), Lucky Poet (an autobiography), pp.41 and 105; The Liverpolitan, January 1934; Liverpool Daily Post Supplement 1927, p.35; Alan Bold (1988), MacDiarmid. Christopher Murray Grieve. A Critical Biography, pp.245, 246, 255, 259, 260.

26. Liverpool Daily Post and Mercury, 11th November 1930, and 15th December 1930.

27. Liverpool Echo, 9th March 1937.

28. Liverpool Scots Society menu 1947.
    Liverpool Daily Post and Echo (1943), Bombers over Merseyside, p.34.

29. Liverpool Echo, 23rd May 1934.

30 Lancs. and Ches. Fed., 1927-1977 (op.cit.)

31. Liverpool Scots Society menu 1947.

32. Lancs, and Ches. Fed., 1927-1977 (op.cit.)
    Information provided by Mr. George Penman.

33. Lancs. and Ches. Fed., Musical Festival Programme.

34. Lancs. and Ches. Fed., 1927-1977 (op.cit.)
    Whitbread Book of Scouseology, Vol. III: Merseyside at Play, (1989), p.29.

35. Lancs. and Ches. Fed., Concert 1952, Programme.

36. Lancs. and Ches. Fed., 1927-1977 (op.cit.)

37. Programme, Highland Ball, 3rd. January 1953.
    Whitbread (1989), Op. cit., p.104.

38. Information supplied by Mr. Tom Graham.

39. Information supplied by Mr. W.G. McKay.

40. Records of Liverpool Battalion, the Boys Brigade.

41. Information provided by Mr. M. Millington.

42. Information provided by Mr. Rob Blackmore

The Municipal Annexe (formerly the Conservative Club) was the venue for Liverpool's
annual Burns Dinner during the late nineteenth century

Liverpool North End Scottish Association had a high profile in local events as this 1927 photograph shows

Wullie Sutherland produced a number of Scottish concerts. His usual pianist Mollie
Munro (nee Carruthers) was conspicuous by her absence on this occasion having given
birth to one of the authors of this book thirteen days earlier

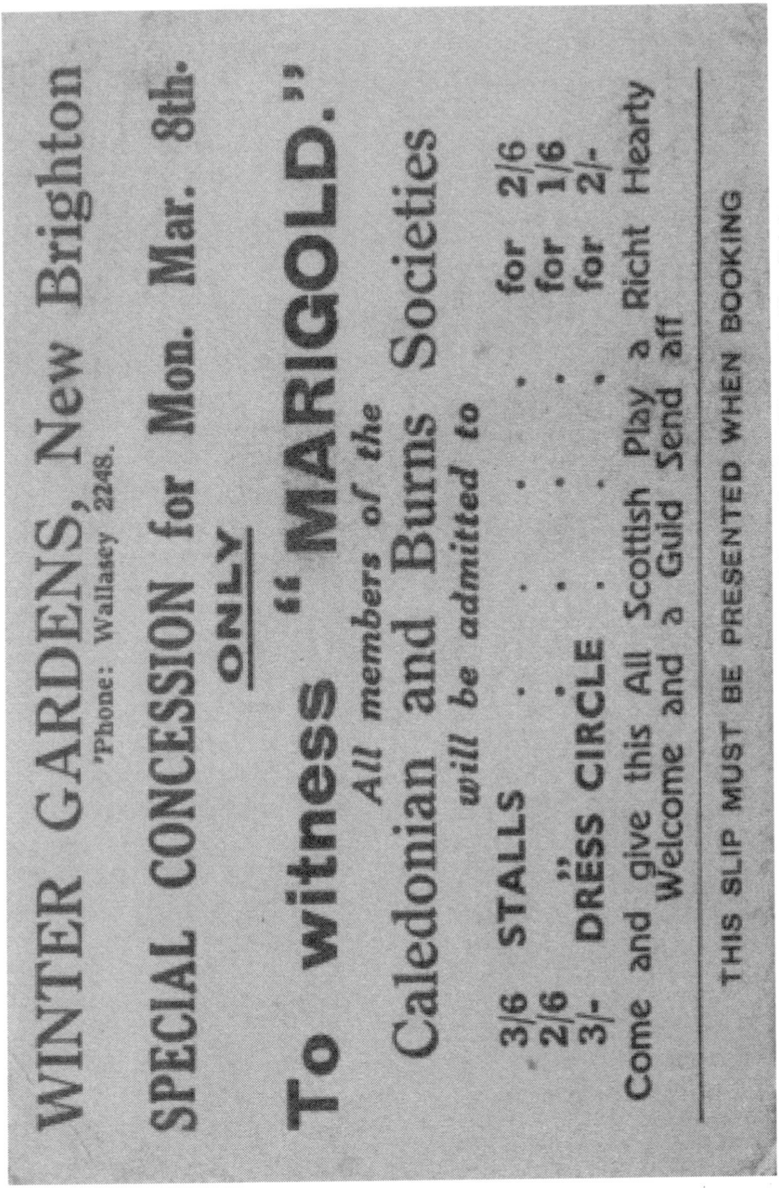

WINTER GARDENS, New Brighton
'Phone: Wallasey 2248.

SPECIAL CONCESSION for Mon. Mar. 8th.

ONLY

To witness "MARIGOLD."

All members of the

Caledonian and Burns Societies

will be admitted to

3/6	STALLS	.	.	.	.	for	2/6
2/6	"	.	.	.	.	for	1/6
3/-	DRESS CIRCLE	.	.	.	.	for	2/-

Come and give this All Scottish Play a Richt Hearty
Welcome and a Guid Send aff

THIS SLIP MUST BE PRESENTED WHEN BOOKING

An invitation to Merseyside Scots from the Winter Gardens Theatre in New Brighton

155

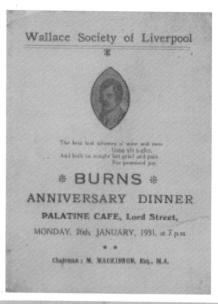

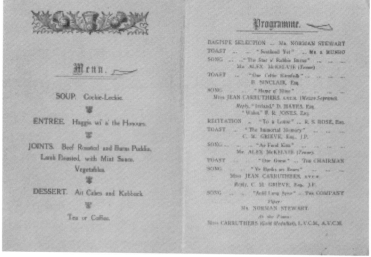

At its annual in 1931, the Wallace Society was proud to welcome C.M. Grieve
(the poet Hugh MacDiarmid) as its guest speaker

There was no idea of informal dress when Liverpool and District Society met for a ramble in the 1920s (Courtesy of Miss N. Wright)

Scottish Concerts were resumed after the war.

158

The modest "Highland Gathering" held at Crawfords Sports Ground in the 1950s grew into the major Highland Games South of the border, now held annually in Blackpool

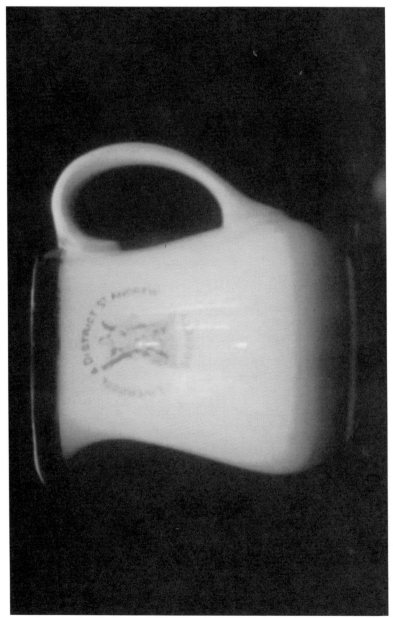

At one time Liverpool and District St. Andrew's Society owned their own crockery

The Annual Clan Macleod Pipe Band Highland Ball
at St. George's Hall was a major event of the 'fifties
Copyright probably Liverpool Daily Post and Echo

Liverpool and District St. Andrew Society. A dinner-dance
in the 1960s at Exchange Hotel

March 1947 at New Brighton Tower when the Scots Societies held a Highland Ball
at which the "Grand March" was a highlight

1968. A celebration of the Lancashire and Cheshire Federation of Scottish Societies. Cutting the cake are Bobby Anderson (Chieftain), Joan Mathias (Secretary), Margaret Sutherland (President extreme left) and Douglas Lauder Foden (Treasurer - Right)

CHAPTER EIGHT

The Scots and Politics on Merseyside

Introduction

During the eighteenth and nineteenth centuries, Scots became increasingly involved in British politics. Colley, for example, refers to the fact that Scots moving to England were increasingly in the position of having fellow countrymen sufficiently highly placed in politics to act as influential patrons [1]. Many Scots, having been actively involved in the Independent Labour Party or the wider Labour and trade union movement, became similarly involved in English Labour politics. Others embraced Scottish nationalism, although this seems to have been less significant. Harvie refers to expatriate Scots as being nostalgic - there were supporters of Jacobitism in both America and Australia in the nineteenth century - or straightforwardly radical, with little time for tradition. He notes that the Scottish National Party has rarely received widespread support from Scots overseas, perhaps in contrast to the Irish [2].

With a substantial number of Scots resident in Liverpool from the early nineteenth century onwards, it is only to be expected that some would become involved in local politics on Merseyside. Given the propensity for expatriates to retain an interest and commitment to their country of origin - as evidenced by the number of Scottish societies in Liverpool - then similarly, it is to be expected that at least some Scots would also become involved in the politics of nationalism, although many would become associated with other political parties. It is perhaps surprising, therefore, that the Scots' political contribution in Liverpool seems to have been slightly limited.

Scots MPs on Merseyside

Although some of Liverpool's Members of Parliament have had Scottish origins, the numbers are small when compared, for example, with those with connections in Ireland. Perhaps the first Scot to sit as MP for the city was the Liberal-Conservative Edward Cardwell, who sat from 1847 to 1852. The son of John Cardwell, a Liverpool merchant, his mother came from Fairlie in Ayrshire. After his defeat in the 1852 election, he returned north to stand, again unsuccessfully, in Ayrshire [3].

Another prominent Liverpool MP was Samuel Smith, who represented the city as a Liberal from 1882 to 1885. He then sat for Flintshire from 1886 until his death in 1906 at the age of 70. Born in Kirkcudbright, and a graduate of Edinburgh University, he was a cotton merchant in Liverpool, becoming President of the

166

Liverpool Chamber of Commerce in 1876[4]. He was a Liberal Councillor from 1879 until 1883 and, as referred to earlier, in Chapter Five, a staunch attender of Canning Street Presbyterian Church. His most lasting monument is the Liverpool Gordon Smith Institute for Seamen, which he established to commemorate his only son, who died of typhoid in 1898. In Parliament, he was a particularly prominent campaigner for the rights of native people in the Empire, for disestablishment of the Church and against the opium trade between India and China.

David MacIver, owner of the steamship company David MacIver and Co. in Liverpool, has already been referred to in Chapter Five. Born in Liverpool but with a Glaswegian mother and Hebridean ancestry, he was, as well as a shipowner, a Director of the Great Western Railway, and of the Fishguard and Rosslare Railways and Harbours Company, and Chair of the Bala and Festiniog Railway. A Conservative, in favour of Tariff Reform, he sat as MP for Birkenhead from 1874 to 1885, when he retired. He returned to politics later, however, becoming MP for Liverpool Kirkdale from 1898 to 1907[5].

The Kirkdale seat was won, in 1907, by Charles McArthur, a Unionist, brought up in Bristol but the son of a Port Glasgow man; he held it for three years. Previously, he had sat for the Exchange division of the city, from 1897 to 1906. McArthur was an average-adjuster (relating to the lading and weighting of cargoes) and, like Samuel Smith, became President of Liverpool Chamber of Commerce [6]. The link between commercial and political eminence is clearly evident.

Across the Mersey, such a link was demonstrated by the Laird family, who were also active in public service and politics. John Laird was Chairman of the Birkenhead Commissioners (the forerunner of the Borough Council) and was both a Justice of the Peace and Deputy Lieutenant of the County of Chester. In 1861, he won the newly formed Birkenhead parliamentary seat for the Conservatives and was returned again at three subsequent elections. His generosity to Birkenhead included provision for the Laird School of Art and the Borough Hospital. His brother William and son John were also JPs and Mayors of Birkenhead. John held the office of Mayor from 1877-79 and again in 1885-86 and William held office in 1880-82 and 1886-87[7].

North Liverpool seems to have attracted several Scots political activists. The Labour candidate for the Kirkdale seat in both of the 1910 General Elections was Alexander Gordon Cameron of Oban. A member of the Amalgamated Society of Carpenters and Joiners, he became a building contractor and in 1917, was appointed by the

Government to sit on an Inquiry into the Industrial and Social Conditions of Scottish Workers. He finally reached Parliament as MP for Widnes from 1929 to 1931 [8].

In adjacent Everton, the Conservative MP from 1892 until his death in 1905, was John Archibald Willox (later Sir John), who was born in Edinburgh. He had moved to Liverpool as a child, however, and was educated at Liverpool College. The son of a journalist, he worked on the *Liverpool Courier* from 1865 onwards, eventually becoming its editor and proprietor. As a journalist, he took an active interest in the political affairs of Lancashire and Cheshire, and became Chair of the Press Association and President of the Institute of Journalists. A strong Unionist, he was President of the National Protestant Union, and was knighted in 1897 [9].

Some MPs were born and educated in Scotland, moving to Liverpool to make their fortune. David Duncan, for example, who was briefly MP for the Exchange division, just before his death in 1886, came from Alyth in Angus and was educated at Dundee High School. He moved to Liverpool in 1849, becoming a successful merchant and shipowner. He was also a Director of the Royal Insurance Company, based in the city, and of British and Foreign Marine Assurance, and other companies. Prior to representing Exchange, Duncan was MP for Barrow-in-Furness, from 1885 to 1886 [10]. He appears in the list of subscribers to the Chair of Philosophy, Logic and Political Economy at University College, Liverpool (see Chapter Five).

There were also Scots who sat for Liverpool parliamentary seats but who appear to have had little connection with the city; the seat may merely have been a convenience. Lord Ramsay unsuccessfully contested a by-election in Liverpool in February 1880, before securing election as one of Liverpool's three MPs in April that year. He sat, however, for less than a year before succeeding his father as Earl of Dalhousie. He had previously been an equerry to the Duke of Edinburgh [11]. Another similar example was William Forbes Mackenzie from Peebles-shire. He was for many years the Deputy-Lieutenant for Peebles-shire and sat as MP for the county from 1837 to 1852. He became MP for Liverpool in 1852 but the election was declared void and he did not contest the subsequent election. He went on to contest Derby in 1857 and died in 1860 [12].

In more recent years, only two Scots have represented Liverpool seats. In 1935, Sir David Maxwell-Fyfe was elected Member for the West Derby division, leaving the Commons in 1954, on his ennoblement as Viscount Kilmuir; in 1962, he was elevated further to an earldom. An Edinburgh man, educated at George Watson's

School, he was a barrister to trade, and in 1945-46, had been Deputy Chief Prosecutor at the Nuremberg Trials. In 1951, he became Home Secretary, achieving notoriety for his refusal to commute the death sentence on Derek Bentley. He was Attorney-General in the last few months of Churchill's government and, as Lord Kilmuir, he served as Lord Chancellor in successive governments, from 1954 to 1962 [13].

Finally, in 1947, the Edge Hill seat was won by Arthur Irvine, later Sir Arthur, who represented the area until his death in 1978. Again from Edinburgh and educated at Edinburgh Academy, he began his political life as a Liberal, contesting Kincardine and West Aberdeenshire in 1935 and 1939. He joined the Labour Party during the War and contested South Aberdeen unsuccessfully in 1946, before becoming the candidate for Edge Hill at a by-election. He became a QC in 1958, was knighted in 1967 and held the post of Solicitor-General from 1967-1970 [14]. In later years, Sir Arthur Irvine's relationship with his Constituency Labour Party was a difficult one and, at the time of his death, they had already decided not to adopt him as their candidate for the 1979 General Election.

Local Political Activism

Some Scots were active in local politics and trade unionism, without actually standing for election. An important character at the turn of the century was Dumfriesshire-born Sam Barton who became a railway clerk in Liverpool. In 1886, he joined the Dingle branch of the Working Men's Conservative Association, becoming secretary in 1900 and a well-known political organiser. In a letter to Lord Derby in 1917, Sir Archibald Salvidge, a prominent Tory Alderman in Liverpool, complained about Barton's methods of working:

> He is a good man in many ways but has absolutely no sense of proportion and is given at times to writing letters which are nothing less than impudent. I have had several of these epistles and on one occasion brought his conduct before the Executive Officers of the Association. The only way to keep him in hand is to have no nonsense and speak to him straight [15].

Barton died, in 1921, aged 61.

Another local activist, in more recent years, was Simon Fraser. The brother of Tom Fraser, Labour MP for Hamilton from 1943 to 1967 and a member of the Wilson government, he was secretary for a time of the Liverpool Trades Council and Labour Party.

As far as Scottish participation in the City Council is concerned, it is difficult to obtain relevant information. Certainly, only one of the city's Lord Mayors has been a Scot, and indeed it is a rarity for anyone from outside Liverpool to have been elected as its first citizen. Alex Griffin was born in Dumfriesshire, beginning his working life in farming but joining the Ayrshire Police in 1904. Five years later, he transferred to the Liverpool force but his career ended prematurely in 1919 when he was one of the prominent leaders of the police strike and was one of many officers subsequently dismissed.

This was his introduction to active politics. In 1921, he became election agent in the Edge Hill constituency, to his former police colleague Jack Hayes; Hayes was the first candidate to win the seat for Labour. In 1928, Alex Griffin entered the City Council, representing Edge Hill ward, becoming a Justice of the Peace in 1941 and an Alderman in 1942.

Griffin's particular interest was in hospitals. For 23 years, he was Deputy Chairman of the Corporation Hospitals Committee and its successor, the Health Committee. He was also a member of four hospital management committees. His public service was recognised when he became Lord Mayor in 1954 [16].

Another key figure in local politics - and something of a local legend - was Margaret Bayne Simey, a Glaswegian who came to Liverpool when her father was appointed Principal of the then College of Commerce (now part of John Moores University). She attended Liverpool University and was its first woman graduate in social science. She has subsequently written a number of books on social conditions, beginning with *Charitable Effort in Liverpool in the Nineteenth Century*, which was first published in 1951 and recently revised, and *Eleanor Rathbone, 1872-1946*. This was a tribute to mark the centenary of the birth of this great member of the philanthropic Liverpool family, which also had links with many Scots philanthropists in the city [17].

Her concern has always been for the disadvantaged and, as Chairman of the Governors of the city's first comprehensive school at Gateacre, fought continually for its interests, even going on site to harangue building workers, when she felt that work on extensions was proceeding too slowly [18].

It is hardly surprising that, in 1963, she was elected to the City Council as a Labour member for Granby Ward, one of the most deprived areas of the city. Despite its deprivation, she lived in the area she represented [19]. She became a JP in 1962 and, in 1974, was elected to the newly formed Merseyside County Council, where she became vice-chairman of the Police Committee. After a short spell when Labour was in opposition (1977-1981), she became chairman and in this position, she continually advocated increased police accountability; her battles with Chief Constable Sir Kenneth Oxford made her a nationally known figure [20].

The abolition of Merseyside County Council in 1986 did not lead to retirement for Margaret Simey and she still, in her 90s, actively supports community projects, especially in Granby. Incidentally, her late husband, who was Professor of Social Science at Liverpool University, was created a Life Peer by Harold Wilson, but Margaret Simey has always discouraged the use of her titles of 'Lady' or 'Baroness'.

Nationalist Politics

The Scots referred to above were active in Liverpool politics and trade unionism, but with UK-based political parties and organisations. During the inter-war period, there were, additionally, Scots living in Liverpool who retained an interest in political issues, specifically related to the growth of Scottish Nationalism. They were unable to stand for election in Liverpool but developed a network of political societies and debating clubs or became active in local trade unions. Mention has already been made, in Chapter Seven, of the Wallace Society of Liverpool, founded in the late 1920s with decidedly pro-Scottish Nationalist sympathies. The precise dates of its operation are unclear but its secretary, Samuel Munro, was still writing letters to the local newspapers in Spring 1935. Munro himself died in 1938 and the Wallace Society is believed to have folded with the outbreak of the Second World War. It does, however, appear in a directory of Liverpool clubs and societies as late as 1949, although this may be inaccurate.

Its origins should perhaps be seen against the background of Scottish politics in the period. The cause of Scottish Home Rule had been espoused by the Labour Party in the period before and after the First World War, by individuals such as Keir Hardie and Ramsay MacDonald but, once Labour took office, other social issues came to be seen as more important for the Party to address. Hardie and MacDonald also represented English constituencies for the bulk of their careers and this deprived them of a Scottish power base. Separate organisations were therefore established in Scotland to pursue the nationalist cause, including the Scottish Home Rule Association, the Scottish National League and various student bodies, notably the Glasgow University. Scottish Nationalist Association. In 1928, they merged to form the National Party of Scotland, becoming the Scottish National Party (SNP) in 1934.

The developments in Scotland were of considerable interest to expatriate Scots and branches of the SNP were established in many places outwith Scotland. The Liverpool branch was founded around 1934 and was in existence until the beginning of the 1950s. Its secretary was Andrew Sim, a native of Aberdeenshire and close friend of Samuel Munro, of the Wallace Society.

Sim and Munro took the decision to make use of the local press to publicise Scottish issues and used all available opportunities to write letters to the newspapers. One of their most ingenious tricks was the invention of the Anglophile A. MacAndrew Fraser whose letters appeared regularly in the columns of the *Liverpool Daily Post* and *Liverpool Echo*, refuting the views of Munro and Sim and mocking the Nationalist cause. One of Fraser's letters would inevitably stimulate Munro or Sim to reply, on behalf of the Wallace Society or the Scottish National Party and the correspondence would continue until brought to an end by a weary editor. In fact, A. MacAndrew Fraser was simply Andrew Sim's 'nom de plume', using his parental address in Birkenhead.

While the correspondence clearly provided some amusement for those involved, the need to invent a figure like Fraser in order to prolong it, may indicate a genuine lack of interest in Scottish nationalism, among other expatriates on Merseyside. It is unclear, for example, just exactly how many members the Liverpool SNP branch actually had and records seem not to have been kept centrally in Edinburgh. Nevertheless, there were high points, notably in March 1935 when prominent Scottish and Welsh nationalists met at a private conference at the city's Adelphi Hotel.

The Duke of Montrose, president of the Scottish National Party, chaired the meeting, accompanied by prominent SNP office bearers from Scotland. The Welsh Nationalists were represented by their vice-president, Professor J.E. Daniel of Bangor, the national organising secretary, J.E. Jones, from Caernarfon, and other members of their Executive. No statement was issued at the end of the meeting, and it is difficult therefore to establish its significance.

Because the Liverpool Branch of the Scottish National Party was operating 'in exile', it was unable to become involved to any great extent in the Nationalist campaigning which was becoming more significant north of the border. Nevertheless, some campaigning was undertaken. During the 1930s, many Scots had had to move south to obtain work, and a number worked on Merseyside, returning home to their families in Scotland at weekends. SNP members began regularly leafleting evening trains to Glasgow, immediately prior to their departure from Exchange Station, drawing attention to the economic circumstances which forced so many Scots to work at a distance from their family homes [21].

After the Second World War, the level of local political activity involving Scots appears to have reduced significantly. The Wallace Society ceased to exist and, although the Liverpool SNP branch continued in existence to the 1950s, it too ceased to function. Individuals, like Andrew Sim, continued to have an interest in Scottish politics but without a formal organisation in place, there was no profile for Scottish interests.

Partly, this may simply have reflected migration patterns, with fewer Scots moving to Liverpool in the post-war period. As shown in earlier sections on population movements, Merseyside ceased to be a significant destination for Scots migrants, who increasingly moved south. The Scottish interest was maintained through the surviving social clubs and societies but they had no political profile.

Conclusion

The contribution by Scots to Merseyside political life has been important, although not spectacularly so. Some Scots have made or extended their careers in politics in the mainstream UK political parties or in trade union activities, while others have focused on nationalist politics, supporting the activities of the developing Scottish Nationalist movement. The level of Scots involvement since the Second World War seems to have declined significantly and there are perhaps three reasons why this has occurred.

Firstly, it is likely that Scots who moved to England to develop their political careers are likely to have done this because of difficulties in doing so at home. This is most likely to have affected the Conservatives. Until the 1950s, all three

UK political parties were significant in Scotland but, from 1955 onwards, the level of support for the Conservatives has fallen dramatically to the point where there are now no Conservative MPs in Scotland. A number of them have looked southwards for new Parliamentary seats but it is unlikely that they have looked towards Merseyside, given the area's strong support for parties of the left. Labour politicians are unlikely to have moved to England because there are plenty of continuing opportunities within Scotland.

Secondly, it seems unlikely that there will be much support on Merseyside for nationalist politics. Quite apart from the declining number of first generation expatriate Scots in the area, the lack of interest in Scottish nationalism amongst expatriates has already been documented by Harvie. He quotes the experience of Arthur Donaldson, later Chairman of the SNP, in trying to raise party funds in America. Writing back, disillusioned, Donaldson suggested that the party should desist from fundraising in future, 'in the United States and the Dominions' [22].

Thirdly, at the time of writing, legislation is going through Westminster, to establish a Scottish Parliament in Edinburgh. Elections to this new Parliament will be held in May 1999 and the Parliament will formally convene in 2000. This will provide new career opportunities for politicians within Scotland but will also mean that, in domestic matters at least, the political and policy concerns of Scotland and England are likely to diverge quite significantly in the future. It may be much more difficult in future years therefore, for Scots (as well as Welsh or Irish) politicians and activists to seek careers south of the border.

References

1. L. Colley (1994), <u>Britons. Forging the Nation 1707-1837</u>, Pimlico, London, p.124
2. C. Harvie (1994), <u>Scotland and Nationalism. Scottish Society and Politics 1707-1994</u>, Routledge, London, p.65 ·
3. M. Stenton (ed) (1976), <u>Who's Who of British Members of Parliament</u>, Vol I (1832-1885), Harvester Press, Sussex, p.66.
4. M. Stenton and S. Lees (eds) (1978), <u>Ibid.</u>, Vol II (1886-1918), pp.331-332.
5. <u>Ibid.</u>, p.233.
6. <u>Ibid.</u>, p.227.
7. D. Hollett (1992), <u>Men of Iron</u>, p.10; Carol E. Bidston (1985), <u>Birkenhead of Yesteryear</u>, pp.30 and 33; material on the Jackson and Laird families held in Birkenhead Library.
8. M. Stenton and S. Lees (eds) (1979), <u>Ibid.</u>, Vol III (1919-1945), p.54.
9. M. Stenton and S. Lees (eds) (1978), <u>Op. cit.</u>, Vol II, p.375.
10. <u>Ibid.</u>, p.104.
11. M. Stenton (ed) (1976), Vol I, pp.322-323.
12. <u>Ibid.</u>, p.252.
13. M. Stenton and S. Lees (eds) (1981), <u>Ibid.</u>, Vol IV, p.252; <u>Dictionary of National Biography</u> (1981), pp.408-9.
14. M. Stenton and S. Lees (eds) (1981), <u>Ibid.</u>, pp.185-186; <u>Who was Who? Vol VII, 1971-1980</u>, (1981).
15. Quoted in P. J. Waller (1981), <u>Democracy and sectarianism. A political and social history of Liverpool 1868-1939</u>, Liverpool University Press.
16. <u>Liverpool Evening Express</u>, 1 April 1954.
17 Jackie Newton (1996), "Tale of the Century", <u>Liverpool Echo</u>, 9 January; Margaret Simey (1988), <u>Democracy Rediscovered - A Study in Police Accountability</u>, p.17.
18. Personal recollection, Alasdair Munro.
19. Margaret Simey (1988), <u>Op. cit.</u>, p.2.
20. <u>Ibid.</u>, p.29.
21. Personal reminiscence, Andrew Sim.
22. C. Harvie (1994), <u>Op. cit.</u>, p.65.

Liverpool and District St. Andrews Society - a dinner in the old Exchange Hotel
(courtesy of Miss N. Wright)

The short lived Highland Society of Liverpool, like the Liverpool Scots Society,
met in the Conservative Club in Durning Road. This photograph was
taken at its first meeting in 1950
(Liverpool Daily Post)

Harold Cook (rear row, extreme left) as well as being pipe major of the Post Office Pipe Band, organised ceilidhs for the Larkhill and Muirhead Tenants Association in the Mansion House, Muirhead Avenue, in the 'fifties

[DIRECTORY.]　　　.OFFICIAL DIRECTORY.　　　2263

SHELTERING HOMES

For Orphan, Fatherless and Destitute Children,

Tel. No. 868 Royal.　　**MYRTLE STREET, LIVERPOOL.**

ESTABLISHED 1872.

Chairman—T. GUTHRIE WILLIAMSON, Esq.
Committee—
A. G. RANKINE, Esq., T. S. HANNAV, Esq., JOHN J. KENNA, Esq., GEORGE McFERRAN, Esq.,
JOSEPH THORBURN, Esq., T. D. PHILIP, Esq., R. B. FORMAN, Esq.
Hon. Secretary—T. N. PHILIP, Esq.
Hon. Treasurer—E. C. THIN, Esq., 24, Chapel Street.
Secretary and Superintendent—Mrs. BIRT.
Bankers—LLOYDS BANK LIMITED.

Over 200 fresh children are received every year. Over 180 emigrated yearly and placed in comfortable homes with Canadian farmers of good standing and repute; 98 per cent. succeed well. Boys received between the ages of 10 and 14; girls between 4 and 16. Cases seen and investigated any week day.

In addition to ordinary school instruction the girls have cooking, laundry and cutting-out lessons, while the boys have carpentry classes and training in the management of horses and cattle.

£12 will defray the cost of emigrating one child.

Funds urgently needed, as many of those who helped to found this institution have passed away.

A 1908 advertisment for Miss Birt's Sheltering Homes

An early Scots' charity, supported by Samuel Smith, was Louisa Birt's Liverpool Sheltering Homes

Part of the war memorial to former pupils of the sheltering Homes. Most had been sent to Canada and fought with the Canadian Divisions

CHAPTER NINE

Conclusions

Introduction: Previous Research

There is now a substantial literature on minority groups within Britain, examining their position from a wide range of angles - political, sociological and economic. But the majority of these studies have tended to have a racial focus, reflecting the widespread migration to the United Kingdom from ex-colonies, from the nineteenth century onwards but particularly in the postwar period. There have therefore been a number of studies in Britain of what came to be called 'race relations' by academics such as Ruth Glass [1] and John Rex [2].

Studies of 'white' minorities are much less common, although there is some work on European and Middle Eastern minorities in Britain, such as Talai's study of the Armenians in London [3] and oral history projects involving Italians and Lithuanians in Scotland [4]. A focus on religious discrimination has led some researchers to examine the experiences of Jewish immigrants and there are studies, for example by Holmes [5], on anti-Semitism in British society. The Irish in Britain have also been the subject of a number of research studies and reference has already been made to work by scholars such as Jackson [6] and O'Connor [7]. Interestingly, however, it is only relatively recently that the Commission for Racial Equality has begun to publish material on the Irish community, although it has long been suggested that the Irish have suffered discrimination in many areas of life [8].

As noted in Chapter One, there has also been some research into Welsh migration into England, by Pooley and Doherty [9], and specific research into Welsh influence on the English building industry [10]. But research into the role played by the Scots in England is curiously quite thin on the ground. Cage's relatively brief chapter in his own edited book [11] is one of the few general accounts, although there are more specific pieces of research instanced elsewhere in this present volume. There is, however, a more substantial body of work on Scots emigration to the colonies and particularly, to North America and Australasia. Donaldson's book on Scots overseas, for example [12], includes an extensive bibliography of specific works on Scots in the United States and Canada, Australia and South Africa. There is a more recent key text by James Hunter on emigration from the Highlands to North America and specifically the experiences of Scots settlers in Carolina, Cape Breton Island and the Quebec/Ontario area [13]. Linda Colley, in her detailed history of British people and the development of the Empire after 1707, identifies the key role played by Scots in the colonies and the way in which Scotland grew prosperous as a result of imperial expansion. It became possible for individuals to be 'British as well as Scottish' [14].

Scots in England

But while the Scottish contribution to Empire was substantial, the role played by Scots in England was equally so. Many Scots emigrated to the New World in search of improved financial and employment opportunities but such opportunities were also present, close at hand, south of the border. Thus, according to Devine,

> Scotland was still a poorer society than England and the difference between opportunities at home and abroad was greater for the Scots. Quite simply, they had more to gain by emigration. The proof of this was the enormous migration from Scotland to England before 1900. For the period 1841 to 1911, according to one estimate, about 600,000 Scots-born persons moved to England and Wales. This was around half of the total net emigration from Scotland in the nineteenth century and was not paralleled by any similar movement from south to the north [15].

Much of this movement was related to fluctuations in the Scottish economy, which was less diversified than England's and was still dominated by heavy, traditional industries. Emigration continued therefore in the 1920s and 1930s, because the interwar slump was more substantial in Scotland. Thus, 'Scots suffered disproportionately and not surprisingly tended to emigrate when they could in greater numbers' [16].

Migration to England was of course significant from all parts of the British Isles and some cities, like Liverpool, became dominated by immigrant communities. Dennis notes [17] that in 1871, only 29 per cent of Liverpool household heads were actually born in the city. A further 12 per cent came from elsewhere in Lancashire and Cheshire but the majority came from further afield, with 24 per cent coming from Ireland alone.

There were, however, important differences between the Irish, Welsh and Scottish communities on Merseyside. The Irish are generally accepted as having been much poorer and many entered relatively lowly paid jobs in England. As a result of these economic constraints, Irish households had little influence in the housing market and often ended up in overcrowded conditions within the inner city. The Irish were culturally distinct from the host society, particularly in relation to religion, the bulk of Irish immigrants being Roman Catholic but also in terms of language, as many immigrants in the nineteenth century would have been Gaelic speakers. The Irish tended therefore to be located in ghettos, spatially segregated from other communities.

The Welsh were not economically constrained like the Irish and were important, not just in the building industry, as identified above, but also in areas like retailing. But the Welsh on Merseyside were usually from North Wales and were often Welsh speaking, especially if families came from Gwynedd. Although the Welsh were Protestants, they were often non-Conformist and there were a number of distinctive Welsh churches established in Liverpool. The Welsh therefore formed a kind of ethnic community, because of their cultural coherence.

The Scots fall somewhere between these two groups. Although Highlanders would be Gaelic speakers, most Scots spoke English. In religious terms, Scots were mainly Protestants, although their faith was Presbyterian rather than Episcopalian like the Church of England. As shown in Chapter Three, there were large numbers of Scots churches on Merseyside and they played an important role in Scottish society in the area. In economic terms, the Scots were generally very successful and Chapter Five describes the major part played by Scots in the commercial life of Merseyside and in particular in the development of shipping companies and the port.

The Scots also had an important professional status and this again helps to distinguish them from other immigrant groups. The significance of Scottish medical training is dealt with in Chapter Four but other professions were represented amongst the migrants. Devine refers to the so-called 'brain drain' as having been a feature of Scottish emigration since mediaeval times:

> Many talented and gifted people left the country even in the eighteenth century which was the great age of Scottish intellectual achievement and remarkable economic improvement.........The exodus of the able has been a constant theme in Scottish history, even in the most dynamic phases of the nation's development [18].

As an expatriate community therefore, the Scots occupied quite a high status and played a significant role in their host society. But while many would have increasingly felt 'British', it was important for them, as Colley points out, to be Scottish as well. Because the Scots, unlike the Irish - or indeed more recent immigrant communities like the Asians or Chinese - did not live in spatially segregated areas, certain institutions became highly significant in helping to maintain this 'Scottishness'. We have already referred to the Kirk. Chapter Seven shows how Scottish societies and clubs played a very prominent part in allowing expatriates to gather together while Chapter Six has described the particular contribution of the Liverpool Scottish regiment. Thus the Scots, unlike many other immigrant communities have not relied on geographical propinquity in order to maintain their distinctiveness and their traditions.

This view would accord generally with the work of Pooley in examining the different communities within Liverpool. Pointing out that the Scots, unlike the Irish, have not located in a 'ghetto', he suggests that:

> Rather, the Scots fall some way between the Welsh and the Irish on the continuum that measures the interaction of socio-demographic and cultural factors. Cultural factors alone do not provide a sufficient explanation as high-status Scots had little contact with working-class Scots and neither was the Scots community so obviously concentrated in a single social class as the Irish. The explanation must lie in a combination of cultural and social factors.......[19].

The preservation of Scottish distinctiveness may also have been quite consciously achieved. Many immigrant groups seek to maintain their identities by being consciously oppositional to their host society; in this way, they can help to preserve their identity [20]. Some individuals, self-consciously Scottish, might determinedly choose marriage partners from the same tradition [21] and this intermarriage, together with communal feeling, has helped to give reality to the notion of a Scottish 'community'. While there is no firm evidence that this has necessarily been the case on Merseyside, nevertheless personal knowledge suggests that some intermarriage has indeed taken place.

The Scottish Community Today

The maintenance of the Scottish community on Merseyside as a distinctive entity will depend on the degree to which assimilation occurs over time. The notion of assimilation implies a process whereby the immigrant group - in this case the Scots - will gradually acquire the sentiments and attitudes of other groups and become incorporated into a common cultural life. The speed at which this process may take place will depend upon the size and distinctiveness of the immigrant group.

We have already seen that the Scots have perhaps been less obviously distinctive than the Irish, with their different religious faith and, unlike more recent migrant groups like the Asians, are not distinguished by the colour of their skin. This might suggest that assimilation of the Scots into a less segregated, more multi-cultural, Merseyside community would occur within one or two generations. A key factor here, however, is whether cultural differentiation might be reinforced with the arrival of new immigrants but this seems increasingly less likely.

As shown in Chapter Two, the influx of Scots to Merseyside has fallen dramatically in the postwar period. This is partly a reflection of declining opportunities on Merseyside and the poor performance of the Merseyside economy, but it also reflects economic changes in Scotland. With the collapse of the old heavy industries and the development of electronics and oil-related employment, the Scottish economy is very different to that of even forty years ago. The political changes within the country reflected in the establishment of the Scottish Parliament in 2000 may mean that emigration will decline, as it has done in the Irish Republic. It seems unlikely therefore that there will be any major influx of Scots to Merseyside in the foreseeable future.

As far as Scottish institutions on Merseyside are concerned, many of the various clubs and societies are still flourishing, although the membership is ageing and newer members are less likely to be first generation Scots. The Liverpool Scottish is no longer a separate regiment and has ceased to be a significant presence on Merseyside. Many of the Scots kirks have ceased to exist and, although there is still a Church of Scotland congregation in Liverpool, it meets within the Western Rooms of the Anglican Cathedral and the former building in Rodney Street is semi-derelict.

The decline in the Scottish presence is visible, at a very simple level, in terms of the social life of the city. As described in Chapter Seven, there were annual Scottish dinners and Highland Balls through to the 1960s and they were a colourful part of the Liverpool social scene. Popular Scottish entertainers visited the city, Andy Stewart and the White Heather Club filling the Royal Court Theatre for a two week stretch, Jimmy Logan touring in Scottish comedy plays. It seems inconceivable that such audiences could be found for similar shows today.

Conclusion

In conclusion, it seems that, like the Scots in Canada and America described by Hunter [22], the Scots on Merseyside will continue to mark their presence by meeting in their clubs and societies and, for a small minority, by attending the Church of

Scotland. Expatriate Scots societies in other parts of the world have survived for many generations and there seems no reason why Merseyside should be an exception.

On the other hand, it seems unlikely that the Scottish community on Merseyside will be renewed by new immigrants and, as it ages, it looks likely to contract. Future generations will probably become more assimilated into the host society and the Scots will become less obviously differentiated from the rest of the local community. It will be interesting to see if devolution and the establishment of the Scottish Parliament will have an impact on emigration in the early years of the next century and it will be valuable to revisit the Merseyside community to examine the impact of these wider political changes.

References

1. R. Glass (1960), <u>Newcomers: West Indians in London</u>, Allen and Unwin, London.
2. J. Rex (1973), <u>Race, Colonialism and the City</u>, Routledge and Kegan Paul, London.
3. V. Talai (1989), <u>Armenians in London. The Management of Social Boundaries</u>, Manchester University Press, Manchester.
4. B. Kay (1980), <u>The Complete Odyssey. Voices from Scotland's Recent Past</u>, Polygon, Edinburgh.
5. C. Holmes (1979), <u>Anti-Semitism in British Society 1876-1939</u>, Edward Arnold, London.
6. J. A. Jackson (1963), <u>The Irish in Britain</u>, Routledge and Kegan Paul, London.
7. K. O'Connor (1972), <u>The Irish in Britain</u>, Sidgwick and Jackson, London.
8. Commission for Racial Equality (1997), <u>The Irish in Britain</u>, CRE, London.
9. C. G. Pooley and J. Doherty (1991), 'The longitudinal study of migration. Welsh migration to English towns in the nineteenth century' in C. G. Pooley and I. D. Whyte (eds.), <u>Migrants, Emigrants and Immigrants. A Social History of Migration</u>, Routledge, London pp.143-173.
10. T. A. Roberts (1986), 'The Welsh influence on the building industry in Victorian Liverpool' in M. Doughty (ed.), <u>Building the Industrial City</u>, Leicester University Press, pp.106-149.
11. R. A. Cage (ed.) (1985), <u>The Scots Abroad. Labour, Capital, Enterprise, 1750-1914</u>, Croom Helm, London.
12. G. Donaldson (1966), <u>The Scots Overseas</u>, Robert Hale, London.

13. J. Hunter (1994), <u>A Dance Called America. The Scottish Highlands, the United States and Canada</u>, Mainstream, Edinburgh.

14. L. Colley (1994), <u>Britons. Forging the Nation 1707-1837</u>, Pimlico, London, p.373.

15. T. M. Devine (1992), 'Introduction: The paradox of Scottish emigration' in T. M. Devine (ed.), <u>Scottish Emigration and Scottish Society</u>, John Donald, Edinburgh, p.12

16. <u>Ibid.</u>, p.13

17. R. Dennis (1984), <u>English Industrial Cities of the Nineteenth Century. A Social Geography</u>, Cambridge University Press, p.34.

18. T. M. Devine (1992), <u>Op. cit.</u>, p.5.

19. C. G. Pooley (1977), 'The residential segregation of migrant communities in mid-Victorian Liverpool', <u>Transactions of the Institute of British Geographers</u> 2, pp.379-380.

20. C. W. J. Withers (1991), 'Class culture and migrant identity: Gaelic Highlanders in urban Scotland' in G. Kearns and C.W.J. Withers, <u>Urbanising Britain. Essays on Class and Community in the Nineteenth Century</u>, Cambridge University Press.

21. M. Gray (1992), 'The course of Scottish emigration 1750-1914: enduring influences and changing circumstances, in T. M. Devine (ed.), <u>Op. cit.</u>, pp.16-36

22. J. Hunter (1994), <u>Op. cit.</u>

There is no longer any indication that this obelisk in Sefton Park is dedicated to Samuel
Smith as the inscription has now been stolen

Detail - the obelisk includes a drinking fountain on either side with an inscription indicative of Samuel Smith's deep religeous convictions - "Whosoever drinketh of this water shall thirst again, but whosoever drinketh of the water that I shall give him shall never thirst again"

The Gordon Smith Institute for Seamen is one example of Samuel Smith's philanthropy

GORDON SMITH
INSTITUTE FOR SEAMEN

(INCORPORATED)

FOUNDED 1820

PATRON: The Earl Mountbatten of Burma,
K.G., P.C., G.C.B., G.C.S.I., G.C.I.E., G.C.V.O., D.S.O., LL.D., D.C.L., D.S.C.

President:　　　The Right Hon. The Earl of Kilmuir, G.C.V.O.

Vice-Presidents:　Lt. Col. The Rt. Hon. The Earl of Derby, M.C., The Rt. Hon. The Earl of Sefton, D.L., J.P., Admiral of the Fleet The Rt. Hon. The Earl of Cork & Orrery, G.C.B., G.C.V.O., The Rt. Hon. Viscount Leverhulme, T.D., J.P., Sir John M. Brocklebank, Bart., Sir Rex J. Hodges, J.P., Admiral Sir Mark Pizey, G.B.E., C.B., D.S.O. †, Sir William Cocker, O.B.E., J.P., LL.D., M.A. Admiral Sir Nigel Henderson, K.C.B., O.B.E.

Chairman: J. A. Nelson, Esq.	*Deputy Chairman:* Rev.Wm. Paxton, F.R.G.S.
Hon. Treas.: W. J. Parry Esq., F.I.M.T.A.	*Dep. Hon. Treas.:* Harry Barnes, Esq., O.B.E., J.P.
Hon. Solicitor: J. E. Hadfield, Esq., J.P.	*Hon. Architect:* H. G. Rowlands, Esq.
Hon. Chaplain: Rev. W. J. Leslie Paxton.	*Hon. Physician:* Dr. G. T. Goodall, M.B., CH.B.

The work is entirely non-sectarian, and interdenominational, and the Society is untiring in all its activities—social, moral and spiritual—for the betterment of Seafarers, their families and dependants, and is entirely dependent upon voluntary support. Residential accommodation, 185 beds in private cabins, amenity rooms, library service, dancing and social facilities. 500,000 meals and beverages served, 50,000 beds per annum.

Secretary and Superintendent: Norman A. Williams, J.P.

Registered Offices:

GORDON SMITH SEAMEN'S CLUB,
-PARADISE STREET　　　LIVERPOOL I.

Telephone:　　　　　　　**Bankers:**
Royal 3003/3004 3005　　The Midland Bank Ltd., 62 Castle Street

A 1930s advertisement for the Gordon Smith Institute

APPENDIX

Scottish Footballers on Merseyside

Introduction

As noted earlier in the text, there has always been a significant group of Scottish sportsmen who have moved to Merseyside at different times in their careers and who have made an important contribution, particularly to the clubs which they have served. Generally speaking, however, the contribution which such men have made to Scottish *society* on Merseyside has probably been relatively less important. In part, this is because their time in the area has often been limited, as they have moved to Merseyside from other clubs, moved on elsewhere, or returned to Scotland at the end of their playing days.

There are some exceptions to this of course. One of the great Scottish internationalists, who played for Liverpool Football Club, was Billy Liddell and he played a prominent part in many aspects of the city's life. He is a prominent member of the Methodist church and always took an interest in Scottish traditions and culture, being elected President of the Liverpool and District St. Andrew Society on two occasions. In 1958, he was appointed a Justice of the Peace for Liverpool and, on reaching the retirement age of 70, he was the city's longest serving magistrate.

In some cases, the families of Scottish footballers who have settled in the area have become prominent in city life. Mention was made in Chapter 7 of the three sons of Alec Raisbeck who were heavily involved in the formation of a Liverpool Scots' Sports Club in the 1930s. Sadly, the venture did not survive.

Finally, some individuals, while remaining involved primarily in football, have had a massive influence on Merseyside over a long period. Kenny Dalglish's shift from player to manager of Liverpool Football club was important as Dalglish was able to use his considerable skills to help the club sustain a period of enormous success at the highest levels.

The following table lists all Scottish football internationalists who have played for Merseyside clubs. In the second column, E refers to Everton, L to Liverpool and T to Tranmere Rovers. The dates in the third column refer to the period when the individual concerned played for Scotland. The final column lists the number of international caps awarded. Brackets indicate that the individual spent part of his international career elsewhere. Thus, Kenneth Campbell played for Liverpool for only part of his career and, of his eight Scottish caps, only three were awarded while a Liverpool player. The sources of information are the *Rothmans Football Yearbook 1998-99*, edited by Glenda Rollins (Headline, London, 1998) and Douglas Lamming's *A Scottish Soccer Internationalists Who's Who, 1872-1986*, (Hutton Press, Beverley, 1987).

Name	Club	International Playing Period	Caps
George Allan	L	1897	1
John Bell	(E)	1890-1900	10 (3)
Dod Brewster	E	1921	1
Kenneth Campbell	(L)	1920-22	8 (3)
Robert Collins	(E)	1951-65	31(6)
John Connolly	E	1973	1
Kenny Dalglish	(L)	1972-87	102(55)
William Dunlop	L	1906	1
James 'Ginger' Dunn	(E)	1925-9	6(1)
Duncan Ferguson	(E)	1992-97	7(3)
Jimmy Gabriel	E	1961-64	2
Gary Gillespie	L	1988-91	13
Torrance Gillick	E	1937-39	5
Andy Gray	(E)	1976-85	20(1)
Alan Hansen	L	1979-87	26
Asa Hartford	(E)	1972-82	50(8)
Tommy Lawrence	L	1963-69	3
Billy Liddell	L	1947-56	28
Stuart McCall	(E)	1990-98	40(11)
James McDougall	L	1931	2
Frank McGarvey	(L)	1979-84	7(2)
Donald McKinlay	L	1922	2
John McNab	L	1923	1
Tom Miller	(L)	1920-21	3(1)
Hugh Morgan	(L)	1898-99	2(1)
Pat Nevin	(E, T)	1986-96	28(8E, 14T)
Steve Nicol	L	1985-92	27
Alex Parker	(E)	1955-58	15(1)
Alec Raisbeck	L	1900-07	8
Bruce Rioch	(E)	1975-78	24(6)
John Robertson	(E)	1898-1905	16(1)
Ian St. John	(L)	1959-65	21(14)
Alex Scott	(E)	1957-66	16(5)
Graeme Sharp	E	1985-88	12
Graeme Souness	(L)	1975-86	54(37)

John Thomson	E	1933	1
Alec Troup	(E)	1920-26	5(1)
John Wark	(L)	1979-85	29(3)
George Wilson	(E)	1904-09	6(1)
George Wood	(E)	1979-82	4(3)
Ron Yeats	L	1965-66	2
Alex Young	(E)	1960-66	8(2)
Sandy Young	E	1905-07	2
Tom Younger	(L)	1955-58	24(16)

Hugh McDiarmid (C.M. Grieve) the Scottish Poet who worked for the Liverpool
Organisation Ltd. for a time

The Liverpool and Manchester Railway Centenary celebrations were organised mainly by Mathew Anderson of the Liverpool Organisation Ltd.

Liverpool Caledonians Baseball Team in mid 1930s
On the front row left is Andrew A. Sim and second
row right (not in sports kit) is Samuel Munro

In the 1940s members of the Liverpool Scots Society celebrated the wedding of one of
their members, Edna Owens, in traditional style. Dave Bruce, Pipe Sergeant of the Clan
Macleod Pipe Band, led the bridal party and guests from St. Cyprian's Church to the
nearby Conservative Club - the meeting place of the Society

A 1906 map Liverpool illustrates the scots influence of one quarter square mile of the city.

1 Oldham Street (Church of Scotland)

2 St. Andrew's, Rodney Street
   (Church of Scotland)

3 Associate Burgher Kirk, Mount Pleasant

4 St. George's, Myrtle Street
   (Free Church of Scotland)

5 Canning Street (Free Church of Scotland)

6 Royal Institution, associated with T.S. Traill

7 Liverpool Institute, associated with T.S.
   Traill

8 Gordon Hall, associated with Samuel Smith

9 The old Philamonic Hall where the scession
   Churches formed the Presbyterian Church
   of England

10 The Liverpool Sheltering Homes

11 Hope Hall where the inaugural meeting of
   the Liverpool Scottish was held in 1902

12 The Approximate site of 8 Hope Street
   where 22 cadavers intended for anatomy
   teaching in Scotland were found.

Col. Graeme Davidson, J.P., the present commanding officer of the Liverpool Scottish

A mystery photograph - As well as a pipe band, the "Scottish" had a military band. THis photograph was taken by a professional photographer in Andover so presumably the "Scottish" was at one of its early camps on the Salisbury Plain

A team of Scottish country dancers entertain at a garden party in Wavertree in the early 'fifties
Left to right are Alasdair Munro (co-author), Ailsa Heeson, Harold Cook (piper), Avril Doig, Pat Jennings and David Fielding

A feature of the Highland Games is weight for height. Jock Hay of Warrington is seen here participating at one of the early Highland Games at Crawford's sports ground, Wavertree, in the early 'fifties

INDEX

208